Cognitive Behavioural Interventions for Mental Health Practitioners

**Edited by
ALEC GRANT**

LearningMatters

First published in 2010 by Learning Matters Ltd

British Library Cataloguing in Publication Data
A CIP record for this book is available from the British Library.

ISBN 978 1 84445 210 1

This book is also available in the following ebook formats:

Adobe ebook: ISBN 978 1 84445 779 3
EPUB: ISBN 978 1 84445 778 6
Kindle: ISBN 978 0 85725 030 8

Text and cover design by Code 5 Design Associates Ltd
Project management by Swales & Willis Ltd, Exeter, Devon
Typeset by Swales & Willis Ltd, Exeter, Devon
Printed and bound in Great Britain by TJ International Ltd, Padstow, Cornwall

Learning Matters Ltd
33 Southernhay East
Exeter EX1 1NX
Tel: 01392 215560
info@learningmatters.co.uk
www.learningmatters.co.uk

FSC
Mixed Sources
Product group from well-managed
forests and other controlled sources
Cert no. SGS-COC-2482
www.fsc.org
© 1996 Forest Stewardship Council

Contents

Acknowledgements

The authors and publisher would like to thank the following for permission to reproduce copyright material.

Dr C Padesky for her layers of belief model (chapter 5).

Drs K Mooney and C Padesky for their five-part model (chapter 5).

Dr Bonnie Spring for her stress diathesis model (chapter 6).

Introduction

Who is this book for?

This book is intended for mental health practitioners from across the range, such as occupational therapists, social workers, nurses, counsellors and medical staff. However, since nurses constitute the largest professional group working in mental health, at one or two points in the book the narrative will focus on this group in relation to the cognitive behavioural therapy (CBT) approach. However, readers from different occupational groups will find that the nurse-focused discussions in the text have relevance for them.

Why cognitive behavioural (CBT) interventions?

We currently live in an era characterised by an increasing need to both know about and justify mental health interventions in regard to their sound evidence base. It is becoming less and less acceptable to provide interventions based either on organisational custom and practice or on theoretical positions which have little or no empirical support.

The contents of this book have a robust evidence base – 'on display' in most chapters – and fully accord with the clinical practice guidelines that can be found on the National Institute for Health and Clinical Excellence (NICE) website (www.nice.org.uk). We therefore think that this text will be both a sensible and a timely choice for readers.

Learning features and book structure

Chapter 1 provides a brief history of CBT and what the approach can offer clients and new practitioners. As well as evidence underpinning the CBT approach, as applied to the range of disorders dealt with in the book, Chapter 2 examines unmet need from the perspective of international and national healthcare and policy. Alec Grant and Gillian Lim explore how this has failed to impact adequately on mental health training and education, how this problem is no longer tenable in the era of Increased Access to Psychological Therapies (IAPT), and how mental health nurse education often remains lacking in an evidence-based curriculum.

Chapter 3 addresses the important topics of client preparation, the first meeting between client and therapist, and the rudiments of CB assessment. Then follow a number of chapters that deal with 'interventions in action'. For all of the disorders covered, the reader is introduced to the problem area, and the evidence-based interventions and case studies which, hopefully, bring these interventions to life.

In Chapter 4, Styliani Gkika introduces the reader to how the CBT approach can help anxious people. After discussing learning and cognitive theories pertaining to the development of anxiety disorders, she goes on to unpack the CB approaches relevant to their treatment. Her discussion then turns to how these approaches can be helpful in specific anxiety disorders: after exploring working with the phobic individual, she invites readers to engage with CBT for panic disorder. Following this, health anxiety is examined, beginning with the CB formulation for this problem area. Obsessive compulsive disorder (OCD) is next discussed and the chapter ends with an examination of how mental health workers using the CBT approach can greatly assist people suffering from post-traumatic stress disorder (PTSD).

Chapter 5 enables the reader to consider how the CB approach can be helpful to people suffering from low mood. In this chapter, Steve Clifford begins by unpacking the meaning of 'depression' and examining its characteristics. The chapter then explores how people become depressed in terms of various theoretical standpoints, including behavioural and cognitive theory. Psychological therapies generally are discussed before the chapter focuses on the role of CBT in the treatment of depression. The types of thinking pattern that can reinforce low mood and depression are explored, and this provides a good basis for an in-depth examination of CBT work with people with these problems. Different ways in which to formulate such problems are discussed in relation to mainstream CB interventions.

In Chapter 6, James Sullivan describes how the CBT approach can help people who hear voices and have false beliefs. He begins with a critique of the 'schizophrenia' concept and then proceeds to examine the role of CBT in helping people with worrying beliefs. This includes a focus on the cognitive attribution style of individuals who hear voices and have false beliefs and some of the problems in engagement and collaboration in working with this client group. The chapter then moves to assessment of this problem area before turning to case formulation of distressing beliefs and related CB interventions.

Alec Grant describes how to help people with Borderline Personality Disorder in Chapter 7. The chapter begins with a brief discussion on how the term 'personality disorder' generally has been used in a pejorative way, as a 'diagnosis of social exclusion', in mainstream mental health services. Following this, the diagnostic criteria for Borderline Personality Disorder are described. The chapter then introduces the cognitive model of personality disorder. The notion of Borderline Personality Disorder as a developmental problem is contextualised in a broader model which takes account of the inherent temperament of the child, genetic factors, childhood development and experience and attachment to significant others in childhood. The general CBT principles and strategies employed in helping Borderline clients are then introduced, in the context of a good therapeutic relationship, and the chapter ends with an illustrative case study which draws on these principles and strategies.

The book draws to a close with a final chapter which invites the reader to consider the important context of workplace preparation for the uptake of CBT. A glossary of the more obscure words, phrases and terms is provided at the very end of the book.

Standards of conduct, performance and ethics in the practice of behavioural and cognitive psychotherapies

Reliance on this book alone would be insufficient to enable readers to practice CBT. The British Association for Behavioural and Cognitive Psychotherapies (BABCP) provides details of all the training courses in the United Kingdom. In addition to adequate training and clinical supervision, provided by a trained and experienced CB therapist, the BABCP (2009) has on its website (www.babcp.com) the following standards of conduct, performance and ethics:

1. You must act in the best interests of service users.

2. You must maintain high standards of CBT assessment and practice.

3. You must respect the confidentiality of service users.

4. You must keep high standards of personal conduct.

5. You must provide (to us and any other relevant regulators and/or professional bodies) any important information about your conduct and competence.

6. You must keep your professional knowledge and skills up to date.

7. You must act within the limits of your knowledge, skills and experience and, if necessary, refer the matter to another practitioner.

8. You must communicate properly and effectively with service users and other practitioners.

9. You must effectively supervise tasks that you have asked other people to carry out.

10. You must get informed consent to give treatment (except in an emergency).

11. You must keep accurate records.

12. You must deal fairly and safely with the risks of infection.

13. You must limit your work or stop practising if your performance or judgement is affected by your health.

14. You must behave with honesty and integrity and make sure that your behaviour does not damage the public's confidence in you or your profession.

15. You must make sure that any advertising you do is accurate.

Chapter 1

A brief history of cognitive behavioural therapy

Alec Grant

C H A P T E R   A I M S

After reading this chapter you will be able to:

- briefly outline the development of cognitive behavioural therapy (CBT) in the second half of the twentieth century;

- understand the role of thinking in human distress and mental health difficulties;

- describe what CBT can offer clients;

- describe what CBT can offer practitioners new to the approach, and what might underpin some initial difficulties;

- consider the relevance or otherwise of the ENB650 case study.

Introduction

In the mid-twentieth century, applied psychology was dominated by the twin edifices of behaviourism and psychoanalysis, represented by the seminal figures of Pavlov and Skinner, and Freud respectively. Behaviourists regarded the inner world of individuals as unimportant, believing that a person's actions were determined and shaped (conditioned) by environmental events. In stark contrast, psychoanalytic adherents believed that the inner world of individuals was all-important. However, equally, they believed that the way the inner world of individuals worked was unconscious, and could only be made accessible with the help of a trained guide – the analyst. The day-to-day conscious thoughts that most people have, and regard as central to their experience of themselves, were viewed by both behaviourism and psychoanalysis as peripheral.

However, there were some lone voices who at that time defended the individual as a conscious agent. Kelly (1955) stressed the way in which individuals seek to give meaning to the world, suggesting that each of us are scientists in regard to our tendency to construct our unique view of reality through a process of experimentation. Ellis (1962) highlighted the significance of irrational beliefs in neurotic disorders, developing rational–emotive therapy (RET) to change these beliefs systematically.

The study of the mental processes that intervene between environmental stimulus and behavioural response is called 'cognitive psychology'. Cognitions, or mental processes, refer to a wide range of activities, including thinking, remembering, perceiving and evaluating or judging. In the 1970s, psychology underwent a 'cognitive revolution' (Mahoney and Arnkuff, 1978). This led to a greater interest in the significance and relevance of cognitive processes to therapy. In large part, this revolution originated in behaviourism in that some investigations were carried out to ascertain how thoughts might be regarded as behaviours, and so might be conditioned or deconditioned just as any other behaviour (Cautela, 1973).

The importance of cognitions in human and psychotherapy process was further developed by Bandura (1977) who showed that it was possible to understand the phenomenon of modelling (learning through observation) from a cognitive rather than a Skinnerian or Pavlovian behavioural perspective. An even more radical departure from, and critique of, behaviourism occurred when attention was drawn to the importance and significance of cognitive processes such as attribution and attention in conditioning (Mahoney and Arnkoff, 1978).

REFLECTION POINT

Based on the chapter so far, write down what you think might be the main implications emerging from the 'cognitive revolution' for helping people with mental health difficulties.

The increasing interest in cognitions resulted in the development of the various cognitive–behavioural therapies. Although they differ in terms of theoretical perspectives, they share common assumptions. This often makes it difficult to distinguish them in clinical practice. The two most influential have been Ellis' rational–emotive behaviour therapy and Beck's cognitive therapy.

This book is exclusively based on Beck's approach, which has been the most extensively researched and seems to be the most popular of the CBTs practised in Britain (see also Grant, et al., 2004, 2008, 2010). The theoretical assumptions that Beckian CBT holds about human beings are (Moorey, 2007):

1. People are active agents who interact with their individual worlds.

2. Such interaction takes place through the interpretations and evaluations the person makes about his or her environment.

3. The results of the 'cognitive' processes are thought to be accessible to consciousness in the form of thoughts and images, and so the person has the potential to change them.

To put the above in practical terms, all feelings and behaviour are mediated by thought processes in the form of personal appraisals and meanings. CB interventions are therefore based on the assumption that any of us may succumb to mental health difficulties if the appraisals or meanings we give to specific events are sufficiently distressing (Grant, et al., 2004). It is usually the case that when we are aware of an impending pleasant event, we usually feel happy and, perhaps, excited. However, if we attached upsetting meanings to events, we are just as likely to experience upsetting emotions. For instance, following a bereavement, a person may feel prolonged and extreme sadness because of a profoundly held belief that they have lost the only person with whom they can feel happy in life. Someone else, who hears personally critical and abusive voices, and thinks that they are true, may well be likely to experience both low mood and anxiety.

Distressing beliefs and feelings are, in turn, likely to influence changes in behaviour. For example, a person who experiences continual sadness, and believes that the future holds no happiness for them, will probably avoid engaging in activities that they previously experienced as enjoyable. Another person who believes that supermarkets are dangerous because of the experience of panic attacks in them is likely to avoid going in them. Equally, someone who both fears and believes the voices they hear may increasingly avoid leaving their home.

From a CBT perspective, the connection of thoughts and emotions with behaviour serves to keep people with mental health difficulties locked into a 'vicious circle'. Within this vicious circle, *what they do* both follows from, and serves to confirm, *what they believe.*

Although this may not happen to all of these individuals, some of them may interpret events as more threatening or personally harmful than they are in reality because of deeply held beliefs and rules for living established at an early stage in life. As will become clear later in the book, in a relatively 'silent' or tacit way, these beliefs and rules influence the ways in which distressed individuals make sense of their day-to-day experiences, the world, and other people (Grant, et al., 2004, 2010).

What CBT can offer clients

As stated above, of all the therapies practised in Britain, Beckian CBT is the most research-based. It must be said that this does not necessarily or logically make it a better approach than any other. However, its research credentials enhance its appeal to discriminating future clients in our increasingly consumer society and will undoubtedly continue to do so. Its evidence base has grown in depth and breadth (Grant, et al., 2004, 2010) which enables us in the CBT community to answer an assured and confident 'yes' to the question 'does CBT work?'

Complementing, and related to, its research base, the highly structured nature of CBT has proved, and will continue to prove, appealing to many clients. Throughout nearly three decades of practice experience, I have come across many clients who have had extremely negative previous encounters with counsellors and therapists offering loose, aimless approaches in mental health services. Approaches which promise the earth, but which lack structure and focus, can leave clients worse off than before. This highlights another positive ethical dimension to CBT: throughout the course of therapy, it is possible for CBT practitioners to specify what they are and will be doing, in what order, and for what reasons.

A further benefit for clients is the psycho-educational nature of CBT. In marked contrast to therapies whose ingredients or strategies are poorly specified, a primary aim of CBT is to teach clients therapy approaches which are closely tailored to their difficulties. Long after formal CBT with their therapist has finished, many clients continue to use the principles and strategies learned in therapy by themselves.

What CBT can offer practitioners new to the approach

ACTIVITY **1.1**

Although you may not want to have formal CBT training right now, if you did at some point in the future, what would be your personal concerns about embarking on such training and what would you wish to gain from it?

Comment

This section will begin by addressing some of the most common, and daunting, personal beliefs in relation to CBT practice that new practitioners have when embarking on CBT training. It will hopefully become evident that having such beliefs does not signal either future incompetence or an inability to be successfully socialised into the CBT practitioner community.

The discussion will then focus on a case study of a group of mental health nurses who trained as CB therapists over a time period from the early 1970s to the late 1990s. As a member of this group, in terms of training and, later, teaching and writing, I am eminently qualified to discuss them. In bringing this chapter to an end, I will talk about their successes and the possible implications of these for individuals undergoing CBT training now and in the future.

RESEARCH SUMMARY

Strong emotions have an adverse effect on thinking. This is known in CBT parlance as 'distorted thinking' or 'cognitive distortions' (Grant, et al., 2004). Cognitive distortions include the following:

- All-or-none thinking *Seeing things in black-and-white categories.*

- Overgeneralisation *Viewing a single negative event as a never-ending pattern of defeat.*

- Mental filtering *Picking out a single negative detail and dwelling on it to the exclusion of other details.*

- Disqualifying the positive *Rejecting positive experiences by insisting 'they don't count'.*

- Jumping to conclusions *This can be either in the form of mind reading or arbitrarily making conclusions about what others are thinking, or fortune telling – predicting that things will turn out badly.*

- Magnification or minimisation *Exaggerating or shrinking the importance of things inappropriately.*

- Emotional reasoning *Thinking that negative emotions reflect the way things really are.*

- Should statements *Criticising oneself and others using unfair rules and standards.*

- Labelling *Calling oneself names in response to events.*

- Personalisation *Blaming oneself or others for something without accounting for other factors that were involved.*

CBT training: The scary early days

Many mental health practitioners engaging formally or informally with the approach for the first time will experience their early days of socialisation to CBT as daunting. It was stressed and illustrated above that from a CBT perspective *thinking* played a central role in psychological distress. This is equally true for novice CB practitioners as it is for clients suffering from mental health difficulties.

Some of the thoughts that novice practitioners frequently suffer from are:

- *I won't be able to do CBT successfully. My colleagues (or fellow students) will, but I won't be able to.*

- *I'm not rational and confident enough. I'm too emotional, and CBT is not for the likes of me.*

- *CBT is too structured for me. I don't like interrupting clients. It's rude.*

The above three appraisals a novice practitioner might make about themselves in relation to CBT should not just be accepted as true. Like all thoughts that give rise to anxiety or low mood, they are distorted. Distorted thoughts are inaccurate and, in a circular way, lead to negative mood states, including anxiety and unhappiness. As they will learn to do with clients, it would benefit novice practitioners experiencing the above appraisals to test out their accuracy in real life, in the form of behavioural experiments.

Taking the first appraisal, *'I won't be able to do CBT successfully. My colleagues (or fellow students) will, but I won't be able to'*. It is hopefully clear that the best way to test this out is in the form of clinical practice with real-life clients. In addition, it would be helpful for novice CB practitioners to explore other areas of their lives where they experience this kind of thinking, and possibly related avoidance, and both apply behavioural experiments to these areas and consider, historically, where this form of thinking style developed from (see Chapters 5–8).

The appraisals *'I'm not rational and confident enough. I'm too emotional, and CBT is not for the likes of me'* and *'CBT is too structured for me. I don't like interrupting clients. It's rude'* are often connected. It's not unusual for emotionally focused individuals, with a high degree of social sensitivity, to feel fearful and unattuned to the practice of CBT because of its perceived valuing of rationality over emotionality and structure over social sensitivity. However, the fact that CBT is structured and values helping individuals learn to re-appraise their thinking does not imply that emotions and relational sensitivity are not a central and important part of its practice. As well as dealing directly with clients' emotional responses in terms of, amongst other issues, what these responses mean to them, trainee CB therapists are encouraged to develop high levels of emotional intelligence and sensitivity, including empathic attunement. Turning to the specific thought *'I don't like interrupting clients. It's rude'*, this is eminently testable. Most trainee therapists who express this thought in clinical supervision are quickly and pleasantly surprised to find out, through the practice of socially sensitive interrupting, that clients do not mind at all and, indeed, often find interruption helpful and containing.

CASE STUDY

The involvement of mental health nurses in CBT: The ENB650 phenomenon

In my experience, training in CBT can confer enormous benefits on individuals, as this last section of the chapter will hopefully demonstrate. The English National Board (ENB) 650 CBT training course ran for around 25 years from 1972 to 1998, in a handful of training centres in Britain. I was a graduate of one of those in the mid-1980s and subsequently went on to become an ENB650 course leader–teacher–practitioner at the University of Brighton.

As well as the production of effective practitioners (Duncan-Grant, 1999a), nurses who undertook the course made a significant contribution to mental health practice. Their small numbers (no more than around 250 in practice at any time from the mid-1970s to the late 1990s) make it all the more remarkable that they pioneered developments in educational leadership, innovation in the development and co-ordination of CBT, applied research, health service management and influential clinical practice (Newell and Gournay, 1994).

In the area of applied research, ENB650 graduates significantly added to the understanding and practice of CBT for depression (Garland, 1996), post-traumatic stress disorder (Lovell and Richards, 1995), chronic fatigue syndrome (Deale, 1997), body dysmorphic disorder (Gournay, 1997) and repeated suicide attempts (Atha, 1992). Others contributed to an increased theoretical understanding of the practice of CBT in organisational contexts (Grant, et al., 2004, 2010) and to the need for the CBT community to develop a greater level of sympathy and understanding for qualitative research approaches (Grant, et al., 2004, 2010).

In addition to the above achievements, three ENB650 graduates held the position as Chair of the British Association for Behavioural and Cognitive Psychotherapies (BABCP), a number were awarded and hold professorial appointments, and several – myself included – achieved the degree of PhD.

CASE STUDY *continued*

Although these achievements are impressive, and hopefully illustrate the possibilities for what some people with a mental health background might achieve, it would be rash to conclude that any group of people could match the above. These achievements need to be placed in context. First, the individuals referenced and referred to above constitute only a small proportion of ENB graduates overall, and so probably represent the most talented, motivated, or both, of the group as a whole. It seems to be the case that, in the main, ENB650 practitioners have ended up spending the rest of their careers, or a considerable part of it, as CB practitioners, and a great many seem to be happy and content in that role.

That said, CB training and education helps individuals develop more of the capacity for an inquiring, analytical mind. This spirit of curiosity can be nurtured to a level where interesting, lively, and relevant research is possible. The nurturance of an inquiring and pioneering spirit perhaps becomes most important when set in the context of unmet need and policy development, the focus of the next chapter.

RESEARCH SUMMARY

Work of Grant, et al.: CBT and qualitative research and related, alternative, forms of writing

a trawl through the mainstream CB journals will confirm to the interested reader that qualitative studies are hardly ever given editorial space. In large part, this is because of . . . 'paradigmatic antipathy' . . . this refers to CB journal boards assuming that qualitative studies are not scientific enough to merit publications . . . An evidence-based agenda amended and broadened to redefine what counts as 'evidence' would . . . repair the 'restricted methodological vision' . . . currently characterising evidence-based CB practice . . . It would speed the paradigm advancement of CB psychotherapy towards an evolving position where the personal meaning-making and narratives of clients and practitioners are accorded much greater respect than is presently the case.

(Grant, et al., 2004, pp230–2)

What other forms of writing are possible that would appeal to a better idiographic understanding of clients and to therapists who respect the intricacies of the therapeutic relationship? As opposed to an over-fixation on the technical-rational, greater credence should be accorded to those process issues in CB psychotherapy which are more difficult to operationalise or to regard as 'outcomes'. It is clearly the case that two clients with what is notionally accepted as the 'same problem' may differ considerably in how the problem was generated, how it is maintained, and how it interacts with their life spaces . . . It would therefore be refreshing if the CBT research literature were to expand to accommodate more accounts, articles and chapters from clients on these issues and on what it is like to experience psychological distress, CB therapy, or, from therapists, on what it is like to provide it. Such a broadened research agenda would, for example, throw light on the possibly differential experiences of both clients and therapists working to a CBT agenda within which what constitutes therapy points more to a psycho-technical enterprise rather than a relationally-focused collaboration in an unfolding therapeutic journey.

(Grant, et al., 2010, p278)

C   H   A   P   T   E   R   S   U   M   M   A   R   Y

The middle of the twentieth century was dominated by behaviourism and psychoanalysis. However, dissenting voices began to pave the way for the 'cognitive revolution' of the 1970s. It was from this context that Beckian CBT emerged as the most extensively researched and popular of the CBTs practised in Britain today. The model of being human proposed by CBT is that people actively interact with their individual lifeworlds, and that such interaction is mediated by the appraisals the person makes about her or his environment. This makes mental ill health a perfectly understandable human phenomenon.

CBT can offer clients the appeal of being evidence-based and structured, with clear procedures that clients can follow and utilise long after formal sessional work with their therapist has ended. Equally, CBT has many advantages to those mental health workers new to the approach. After tackling initial problems of engaging with CBT, often mediated by dysfunctional thinking, novice therapists may well experience themselves developing a keen, inquiring, analytic mind. In the past, this has led to some CB therapists becoming researchers, academics and writers, who have contributed to the knowledge base of the field.

FURTHER READING

Grant, A, Mills, J, Mulhern, R and Short, N (2004) *Cognitive behavioural therapy in mental health care.* London: Sage Publications Ltd.

This text contains excellent chapters on organisational factors impacting cognitive behavioural practice, a critique of evidence-based mental health in relation to CBT and the need for qualitative research to inform CBT practice.

Grant, A, Townend, M, Mulhern, R and Short, N (2010) *Cognitive behavioural therapy in mental health care.* 2nd edition. London: Sage Publications Ltd.

Building on work in the 2004 text above, this book has a chapter devoted to a critique of the philosophy of science underpinning CBT practice and the related need for first-hand accounts of the experience of therapy from clients and the experience of doing therapy from CB therapists.

USEFUL WEBSITES

www.octc.co.uk

This is the site of the Oxford Cognitive Therapy Centre. It is an excellent resource for training and supervision information, and for publications.

Chapter 2

Unmet need: Policy and related recommendations

Alec Grant and Gillian Lim

C H A P T E R   A I M S

After reading this chapter you will be able to:

- understand the reasons for the international and national need for evidence-based healthcare;

- understand the need for cognitive behavioural provision in Britain;

- debate the dissemination of cognitive behavioural approaches as a moral imperative;

- understand the models of cognitive behavioural implementation, specifically high- and low-intensity working, within a stepped care model;

- consider the extent to which evidence-based psychotherapy can meet evidence-based mental health nursing.

Introduction to conceptual background

This chapter will introduce readers to the international and national need for evidence-based healthcare. Following this, the discussion will focus on CB provision in Britain. The question will then be posed: is the dissemination of CB approaches a moral imperative for British mental healthcare workers? Readers will be introduced to current models of CB implementation, constituting high- and low-intensity working within the Increased Access to Psychological Therapies (IAPT) project.

The discussion will then turn to the interface between evidence-based psychotherapy and evidence-based mental health nursing (given that mental health nurses constitute the largest professional group in psychiatric treatment and care). In order to address this issue, the recent mental health policy picture will be presented in relation to traditional forms of mental health nurses' therapeutic engagement with their patients and clients. It will be argued that there has been a long-standing gap between therapeutic theory and nursing practice, and policy drivers aimed at changing this state of affairs will be introduced. The overall picture emerging will be stated as one of a constant failure of mental health nursing to embrace and implement evidence-based therapeutic practice. Some possible reasons will be given to explain this failure.

Finally, the past and current use of the CB approach in British mental health nursing will be revisited and a future vision for British mental health nursing, and generic mental health workers, in relation to the approach will be described.

> ### ACTIVITY 2.1
>
> Do an internet search on evidence-based healthcare. Identify its historical development and its links with mental health. Discuss as a group.

The international and national need for evidence-based mental healthcare

In the early years of the twenty-first century, it is becoming increasingly difficult to justify the provision of non-research-based forms of mental health interventions internationally. The CB approach to helping individuals with mental health problems is thoroughly evidence-based. For a decade or more, support for its provision can be seen in an ever-growing range of mental health problems where it has been found to be helpful (Barlow, et al., 1999; Nathan, et al., 1999). This range includes anxiety-based problems and depression (Department of Health, 2001; Hawton, et al., 1989; Leahy and Holland, 2000; Wells, 1997) and severe and enduring psychoses (Gamble and Brennan, 2000; Grant, et al., 2004, 2010; NICE, 2008).

However, in spite of the evidence for the effectiveness of cognitive behavioural interventions, many individuals suffering from mental health difficulties throughout the world are unable to access the help that they require (Andrews and Henderson, 2000). Undoubtedly, this problem has been created by the increasing costs of healthcare internationally (Rachman, 1996). Aside from economic problems, however, prejudice has been evident in mental health nursing care, with CB approaches often seen as prescriptive, mechanistic or, indeed, brutal (Clarke, 1999; Duncan-Grant, 1999b).

It is also likely that, both in clinical practice and in education, many mental health professionals worldwide operate on the basis of 'custom and practice' or theoretical orientations other than those governed by empirical research. It will be argued below that mental health provider organisations may tacitly collude with a trend of services maintaining a nursing practice status quo that disadvantages service users (Grant and Mills, 2000; Grant, et al., 2004, 2010).

A final problem is that many mental health workers are understandably distrustful of the claims made in the name of evidence-based practice (Barlow, et al., 1999; Bolsover, 2002; Brooker, et al., 2002; Holmes, 2002) because of particular controversies associated with the concept (see Grant, et al., 2004, 2010 for further reading on this topic).

Cognitive behavioural provision: The British scene

Towards the end of the twentieth century, it was recognised that mental health practitioners in the United Kingdom desperately needed training in cognitive behavioural therapy (DoH, 1999). Reflecting a trend in the rest of the world, this was because the public-sector provision of effective interventions for users of mental health services had been grossly inadequate to date. In this context, the National Service Framework for Mental Health stressed the urgency of expanding the provision of evidence-based training and education in mental healthcare generally, to include cognitive behavioural interventions specifically (DoH, 1999). It was envisaged that such provision would enable practitioners to respond appropriately to individuals with 'common' mental health problems encountered in primary care. This was seen to include people with anxiety- and mood-related disorders and individuals suffering from psychotic problems.

In 1998, the British Department of Health called for a greater investment in staff training to support this modernising agenda, to ensure that effective interventions would be offered where they were most needed and would be likely to achieve the most impact (DoH, 1998). In line with this policy, a study conducted by Brooker, et al. (2002) aimed to map university-accredited, post-qualifying training and education for mental health professionals in England, to equip them to work with people with serious mental health problems. Sadly, amongst a raft of other findings, Brooker and his colleagues reported that, in university mental health teaching departments, the provision of training and education in evidence-based practices generally, and in CB approaches specifically, seemed to be the exception rather than the rule.

REFLECTION POINT

Consider the extent to which the mental health interventions you witness in your practice areas can claim to have an explicit evidence-base.

Then, follow up this discussion with conversations with your mentors in practice about their views on this.

Dissemination of CB approaches: A moral imperative?

ACTIVITY 2.2

Access the NICE website (www.nice.org.uk) and search for 'mental health problems'. Identify the number of times cognitive behavioural therapy is mentioned for specific mental health problems.

The overall importance of evidence-based psychological therapies has been accorded a high profile in policy literature in the last decade (see e.g. DoH, 1996, 2001, 2004). CB approaches remain consistently the 'front runner' in this context. This is reflected in clinical practice guidelines in the National Institute for Health and Clinical Excellence website (NICE, 2008), with British mental health nurses constituting the largest professional group in the overall dissemination agenda (DoH, 2006). Since the publication of the *Depression Report* (Centre for Economic Performance, 2006), and the Labour Government's manifesto commitment in 2005 to increase the psychological treatments available to those suffering from anxiety and depression, the more recent pioneering development of both demonstration and pathfinder project sites, and the government's current investment of £173 million pounds to better cater for the common emotional difficulties of anxiety and depression, the profile of the CB approach has arguably never been higher (DoH, 2007a, b, c).

ACTIVITY 2.3

Access the following website:

http://cep.lse.ac.uk/research/mental health

Find out as much as you can about The Depression Report *and discuss its implications as a group.*

Models of cognitive behavioural implementation: Low- and high-intensity working

Within the Increased Access to Psychological Therapies (IAPT) project (CSIP, 2009), the models of CB implementation envisaged in policy define two levels of practitioner within a stepped care model. This project and model is aimed to train mental health workers to help individuals with anxiety and depression of various severities. The levels of practitioner are described as low-intensity and high-intensity workers, both of which are trained in a massive higher educational programme rolled out in 2008. The vision is that low-intensity workers will mainly monitor medication and case manage depression, with a focus on behavioural activation (see Chapter 4) and problem solve therapeutic interventions. Low-intensity work with people with anxiety disorders will still regard case management as important. However, there will be more of an emphasis placed on brief psychological interventions such as exposure and related CB interventions. As part of the low-intensity pathway, mental health clients will also be offered computer-assisted CB therapy (CCBT) (DoH, 2007c) or other supported self-help materials.

The vision for the high-intensity worker is threefold: first, to work with clients who have not responded to the first line of therapy with a low-intensity worker; second, to work with clients who were screened out of the low-intensity pathway due to their difficulties being too severe or too chronic; third, to have a crucial role to play in supervising low-intensity workers.

In supporting the low- and high-intensity practitioners, it is envisaged that mental health services are set up with supporting clinical pathways, systems and processes to ensure rapid assessment and implementation of the protocols, with assertive follow-up of clients referred to the respective services.

The above model was tested in two pilot projects in Newnham and Doncaster and emergent results showed that good outcomes were being achieved (Richards, 2007). Following this the models were further used in pilot work in another ten sites in England. These further sites aimed to learn more from the process to inform policy and apply the model to wider client groups, including the elderly and child and adolescent services (Richards, 2007).

By 2007/8, in anticipation of the imminent translation of policy to practice, and following earlier policy work regarding counselling and psychotherapy services (DoH, 1996), many Trusts began to develop psychological therapy services organised on a stepped care basis. Evidence-based stepped care within healthcare has two key aspects. The first of these, and the one which equates with low-intensity workforce development in psychological therapies, is that the amount of therapist time utilised is limited but focused around psychological interventions that the evidence indicates will provide significant psychological health gain.

In stepped care, more intensive treatments are then reserved for people who do not benefit from the simpler first-line interventions, or for those people where it can be accurately predicted that no or limited benefit will be derived from the first-step interventions. The second important feature of stepped care is that the system must be self-correcting. This means that the outcomes of therapy must be closely monitored and case managed in order that the interventions are stepped up if health benefits are not being released with lower-intensity interventions.

Thus stepped care is a rational evidence-based and economic approach to psychological therapies delivery that its exponents argue has the potential for deriving the greatest benefit from available therapeutic and economic sources. Policy also emphasises that the worker roles (high- and low-intensity workers) in the mental health services should have defined competencies rather than have allegiances, or be aligned, to specific profession groups or specific academic levels of preparation (DoH, 2007a).

Can evidence-based psychotherapy meet evidence-based mental health nursing?

As mentioned earlier, mental health nurses constitute the largest professional grouping in mental healthcare work. It is inevitable that evidence-based psychotherapy, specifically CB therapy, will impact mental health nursing. However, in order to identify in what ways this will occur it is necessary first to examine how nursing policy and practice have developed in recent years and the obstacles for mental health nurses in achieving competence and confidence in CB therapy.

The mental health nursing policy picture

The integration of Carl Rogers' ideas in mental health nursing policy and practice

Historically, mental health pre-registration curricula has embraced and attempted to integrate the ideas and values of Carl Rogers in the teaching of subjects such as basic counselling skills (Egan, 1986; Tschudin, 1987) and Six Category Intervention Analysis (SCIA) (Heron, 2000). It has been assumed throughout the years that at the end of the pre-registration programme the mental health nurse will be able to demonstrate knowledge and competence in applying these basic skills. It is important at this point to alert readers to the fact that the debate about whether the Rogerian core conditions are both necessary and sufficient to result in positive therapeutic change for clients rages on in therapeutic circles.

ACTIVITY **2.4**

Access The British Association for the Person-Centred Approach website:

www.bapca.org.uk

Follow as many links as you want, but check out current and recent research activity.

What are your views, collectively or individually, on the sufficiency of the person-centred approach on its own to produce positive therapeutic change among your patients and clients?

The gap between theory and practice

In spite of the above assumptions, it has long been recognised that there exists a theory-to-practice gap in mental health nursing (see e.g. Bendall, 1976). This gap has continued despite reforms in education (UKCC, 1986) which were intended to positively address the theory-to-practice issue (Maben, et al., 2006). Project 2000 (P2K), for instance, has been criticised over the years for failing to produce nurses fit for practice. These criticisms have essentially focused on the ability of the P2K programme to produce nurses able to meet the challenges of modern mental healthcare (UKCC, 1999).

The emergence of the importance of evidence-based interventions

A review of the P2K programme led to a greater focus on communication. More significantly, new modules on psychosocial interventions were added. However, the organisation and implementation of these changes have tended to vary between training institutions. The document *Fitness for Practice* (UKCC, 1999) highlighted the need for evidence-based practice and competency-based programmes to redress the long-standing imbalance between knowledge and skills. However, the issue of mental health nurses' inadequate practice skills once again came under scrutiny in the following contemporary drivers for changes to mental health nurse education.

Drivers for change in the education of mental health nurses

Recent years have seen the emergence of a number of policy documents that have put mental health at centre stage. These include the *National Service Framework* (DoH, 1999), and *The Capable Practitioner* (SCMH, 2000).

All of the above policy drivers have aimed to generate a change from traditional practice to the development of modernised mental healthcare. What follows is a brief discussion on key additional documents which have a crucial bearing on attempts to change the face of mental health nurse education.

Following the publication of *Fitness for Practice* (UKCC, 1999), the Common Foundation Programme (CFP) was shortened to one year, with the remaining two years of the overall programme functioning as the mental health branch-specific programme. Perhaps more significantly, the shift in the conceptualisation of the mental health 'patient' to that of 'service user' was hoped to lead to a new, more balanced, view about nurse–client relationships (DoH, 1994). In the past, the relationship between a mental health 'patient' and mental health nurse was not based on an equal partnership in that the patient's role was passive and played little part in contributing to an individual's own nursing care and medical treatment programme (O'Carroll and Park, 2007).

The *Knowledge and Skills Framework* (KSF) (DoH, 2004) has put the importance of 'application of knowledge and skills' at the heart of the movement to improve the quality of interventions for service users within the NHS. This emphasis on the application of knowledge and skills, rather than the possession of knowledge, may serve to narrow the theory-to-practice gap. By setting a template that breaks down needed skills into core and specific dimensions, the KSF not only enables individual nurses to become more aware of their existing knowledge and skills, but also provides them with the opportunity to identify their own learning and developmental needs as they progress in their career. Equally, for employers, the framework has aimed to support the pairing of nursing roles with skills, thus avoiding role conflicts between staff. In ideal terms, the KSF also serves as a platform for closer partnerships between healthcare organisations and their workforces.

The Chief Nursing Officer's (CNO) review (DoH, 2006) emphasised the urgent need to provide a modernised, mental health nursing service. Within this, a mental health nursing workforce was envisaged that was capable of employing evidence-based interventions competently in order to improve service outcomes. This drive to modernise mental health nursing has increased momentum in recent years for a number of inter-related reasons, to be discussed further below. It should be remembered at this point that evidence-based interventions, within which the CB approach is the front runner, are high on the government's agenda.

The failure of mental health nurses to embrace and implement evidence-based practice and some possible reasons

The new ways of working with service users promised by the above policy documents clearly raised new challenges for mental health nurses, used to traditional mental health nursing practice, and set the impetus for change in the education of mental health nurses. This was supported by the CNO's emphasis on the need for evidence-based approaches to care through a transparent partnership between education and service providers. However, the CB approach was not explicitly mentioned in the CNO report and is currently not a requirement in pre-registration programmes. Equally, there are no clear guidelines provided for qualified mental health nurses to be proficient in applying the approach.

In spite of attempts to address this state of affairs (Newell and Gournay, 2000), there is little or no evidence in existence that evaluates the effectiveness of mental health nursing interventions (Haque, et al., 2002; O'Carroll and Park, 2007). Indeed, Short, et al. (2004) pointed out that mental health nurses continue to use non-evidence-based interventions such as providing reassurance to anxious clients, when the available evidence strongly suggests that this kind of intervention constitutes safety-seeking behaviour (Salkovskis, 1996) which could reinforce and maintain anxiety (Salkovskis and Warwick, 1986; Salkovskis, 1996).

The existence of the above forms of ineffective practice might relate to the fact that the process of improving service outcomes for clients has been piecemeal, which may continue to reinforce and maintain the inertia within mental health nursing.

However, some of the problems for the failure of mental health nurses, and other mental health workers, to grasp the nettle of evidence-based practice may lie in the nature of practice organisations themselves (see e.g. Grant and Mills, 2000; Maben, et al., 2006). It is the case that many qualified mental health nurses spend minimum contact time with their patients and clients (Clarke and Flanagan, 2003; Whittington and McLaughlin, 2000), limiting the opportunity either to build a relationship with their clients or to work therapeutically. This may be because nurses simply do not have the time to fulfil their therapeutic role. However, more fundamental problems may lie in the nature of bureaucratic organisations.

RESEARCH SUMMARY

Goffman (1969) analysed the process of meaning-making in organisational life using the metaphor of the stage. He argued that 'frontstage' activity is public and subject to scrutiny, thus must be carefully scripted and crafted to satisfy public need. 'Backstage' activity, on the other hand, is more relaxed: organisational 'actors' can take off their masks and be themselves, even to the point of criticising their frontstage acts.

Meaning-making in organisations is characterised by the appearance of frontstage rational activity devoted to the client groups the organisation purports to serve. This is reflected in public statements of mission and purpose. However, in reality, this rational front is always inevitably related to, and threatened by, an emotional backstage (Fineman, 1996).

The emotional agenda of organisations can be played out in various forms of staff resistance. This agenda also takes the form of various ways of influencing the behaviour and attitudes of organisational members (Fineman, 1996), carried out at both organisationally conscious and unconscious levels (Morgan, 1997), in the service of the maintenance of organisational custom and practice (Pfeffer, 1981; Purser and Cabana, 1998). In turn, this may result in innovations to practice, such as the CB approach, being seen as a threat to the 'way things are done around here'.

The past and current use of the CB approach in mental health nursing in Britain

As described in the previous chapter, relatively small groups of specialist mental health nurses have been thoroughly trained in CB therapy since the early 1970s (Newell and Gournay, 1994). However, these 'nurse therapists' tend to work within specialist environments, separate from their generic mental health nursing colleagues. These environments may include departments of clinical psychology or departments solely composed of, so-called, nurse cognitive behavioural therapists.

It could be argued (Grant, et al., 2004) that these specialists are only special at the expense of the vast majority of their generic colleagues who are not. This may reinforce the perception of many mental health nurses that the CB approach can only be applied by specialist nurses.

One possible 'economy class' response to this position is to dedicate CB study days for generic mental health nurses and other workers. This attempt to encourage them to use CB skills in their day-to-day practice may be seen to constitute a useful start in training them up. Equally, such initiatives may simply start and end with providing a basic CB service to a large group of people at lower cost and quality.

A further problem is that such minimally CB-trained nurses are often in danger of being left to practise in an unsupervised way, unsure if they are making a difference to the practice. This may further reinforce the idea that only specialist-trained CB nurses can use the approach while generic mental health nurses cannot.

A future vision for mental health nurses, and other mental health workers, in relation to the CB approach

Beck's vision of the future of the CB approach, as reported by Padesky, (cited in Grant, et al., 2004), is that evidence-based interventions will become the normal, accepted form for those using psychotherapeutic approaches for all those workers who attempt to help people with mental health problems. In a conversation with Padesky (see Padesky's foreword in Grant, et al., 2004), Beck drew attention to the fact that Carl Rogers' ideas of 'warmth, empathy, transparency and non-judgemental positive regard' had become integral to all psychotherapeutic approaches directed to helping people with mental health problems. In his view, they are clearly no longer regarded as stand-alone concepts only applicable to person-centred therapy.

Ironically, how Rogers' ideas and values contribute to effective interventions is difficult to substantiate, and approaches such as Six Category Intervention Analysis (SCIA) (Heron, 2000), which lack rigorous testing for their effectiveness, continue to be taught within the mental health nursing curricula. In contrast, the CB approach is one of the most tested, scientifically underpinned and effective psychological therapy approaches. It is recommended as one of the first-line interventions for mental health problems such as depression and anxiety (NICE, 2008). However, as previously stated, the teaching and inclusion of the approach in the pre-registration curricula is, at best, in its infancy stage and, at worst, non-existent.

It seems logical to propose, in the face of the development of partnership policy in the last decade, that a CB-based mental health pre- and post-nursing curricula will provide a strong foundation in the development of a future mental health nursing workforce. This will meet the needs and improve the experience of mental health service users and their carers. The majority of the generic population of mental health nurses, and other workers, cannot continue to be sidelined from having the opportunity to learn the basic principles of the CB approach and to develop their expertise and knowledge of the approach through appropriate clinical supervision. Neither can the key players in higher education and the service sector continue to ignore the possibility of making a real difference in the development of a modernised, contemporary, mental health workforce.

In summary, mental health nursing and, arguably, the generic mental health workforce is desperately in need of a thorough revision which places the CB approach at the heart of a modernised, evidence-based curricula. Adopting the approach in a supervised way, by high- and low-intensity CB workers will enable mental health nurses and others, upon qualifying, not just to be able to demonstrate basic communication and interpersonal skills but also to work effectively with service users and their carers.

C H A P T E R   S U M M A R Y

It has become increasingly difficult to justify the provision of non-research-based forms of mental health interventions, internationally, in the early years of the twenty-first century. There is now ample support for the provision of cognitive behavioural interventions for a growing range of mental health difficulties. In spite of this, many individual throughout the world are unable to access the help they require. This is due to the increasing costs of healthcare internationally, the failure to relinquish custom and practice for evidence-based practice, and prejudice on the part of some occupational groups where the CB approach is often seen as prescriptive or mechanistic.

However, the National Service Framework for Mental Health in Britain has stressed the urgency of expanding the provision of evidence-based mental health education. This is reflected in the high profile accorded to evidence-based psychological therapies in the policy literature in recent years, resulting in the Increased Access to Psychological Therapies project and stepped care interventions.

The policy- and evidence-based importance of CBT has not, to date, been reflected in the modernising of mental health nursing agenda, following the Chief Nursing Officer's (CNO) review. There remains little or no evidence in existence that evaluates the effectiveness of mental health nursing interventions. However, small groups of specialist mental health nurses, thoroughly trained in CB approaches, have thrived in British mental healthcare for almost four decades. While this may reinforce the idea that CBT can only be carried out by occupational specialists, equally, a CB-based mental health pre- and post-nursing curricula will hopefully provide a strong foundation in the development of a future mental health nursing workforce.

FURTHER READING

Grant, A, Mills, J, Mulhern, R and Short, N (2004) *Cognitive behavioural therapy in mental health care.* London: Sage Publications Ltd.

This eminently practical book uses the international and national healthcare need as a rationale and basis for practical chapters which describe and discuss CB interventions in relation to a comprehensive range of mental health difficulties.

Grant, A, Townend, M, Mills, J and Cockx, A (2008) *Assessment and case formulation in cognitive behavioural therapy.* London: Sage Publications Ltd.

Building on the 2004 book above, this text explores assessment and case formulation in great depth. After doing so, the assessment and case formulation principles are applied to a range of client-centred case studies.

Grant, A, Townend, M, Mulhern, R and Short, N (eds) (2010) *Assessment and case formulation in cognitive behavioural therapy.* 2nd edition. London: Sage Publications Ltd.

This second edition text will bring readers more up to date with developments in CBT, introducing them to state-of-the-art chapters by world leaders on, for example, Bipolar Disorder and Borderline and Antisocial Personality disorders.

Greenberger, D and Padesky, CA (1995) *Mind over mood: Change how you feel by changing the way you think.* New York: Guilford Press.

This is a classic self-help text, mainly focusing on depression and anxiety disorder. Although it may appear old, it is by no means dated. One of its major strengths lies in helping mental health workers wishing to use the CBT approach explore their own difficulties. Self-exploratory exercises throughout the book enable the reader, among other things, to become familiar with their own core beliefs, rules for living and automatic thoughts, and how all of these can become activated.

Newell, R and Gournay, K (2000) *Mental health nursing. An evidence-based approach.* London: Churchill Livingstone.

This text might be useful to mental health nurses and other readers make the link between CBT and other evidence-based approaches.

USEFUL WEBSITES

www.padesky.com

This website, of the famous North American Cognitive Therapist, Dr Christine Padesky, is a treasure of information about the cognitive behavioural approach. It includes many free downloads and very reasonably priced resources, such as training CDs and DVDs.

www.babcp.com

This is the website of the British Association for Behavioural and Cognitive Psychotherapies, the leading organisation for practitioners of the cognitive behavioural approach in Britain. It is a rich source of information, including training events and information about accredited practitioners, trainers and supervisors of the approach.

www.octc.co.uk

This is the website of the Oxford Cognitive Therapy Centre. Training events are advertised as are many very accessible cognitive behavioural self-help books for clients and mental health practitioners.

Chapter 3
Client preparation and assessment

Alec Grant

C H A P T E R A I M S

After reading this chapter you will be able to:

- outline the importance of preparing the client for CBT;
- outline the importance of the referral process;
- assess the first encounter the client has with CBT;
- understand the rudiments of assessment.

Preparing the client

The steps needed to prepare clients for CBT will vary according to the social context that they present for help. For example, clients who come from social environments generally hostile to outside 'authority' figures may need quite a bit of time and informal exposure to CBT ideas and CBT practitioners before their formal referral. This picture contrasts markedly with the middle-class client who already has an investment in the benefit of psychotherapy prior to formal referral to CBT services.

All clients should be referred on the basis of informed consent. This means that they are given verbal and also written information about the CB approach and what it might have to offer them. They should then be given time to think about the referral, if such time is needed, before the referral is made. The referral letter to the CBT practitioner or service should contain accurate information about the client that will help in the process of CBT assessment.

For primary care clients, all the above is what *should* happen. Most of the time, the referral process approximates sufficiently to what has been described so that the client and therapist can embark on the CBT assessment process with goodwill on both sides. However, 'referral baggage' is a danger for clients in primary care (and in secondary care as will be described below). At worst, clients can be referred without being aware of the fact, and because of this turn up perplexed, and often angry, for their first CBT assessment session. The CB therapist has little choice then but spend the session debriefing the client rather than engaging them in assessment.

This problem of what might usefully be described as 'referral etiquette' is often linked to 'referral misinformation'. Misinformation is often given in the context of rushed referrals, where, for example, general practitioners assume that the client has a particular problem when indeed they have not. Consistent trends in referral misinformation can often be identified over time among referrers who might have difficulty distinguishing agoraphobics from aardvarks!

Such referral problems in primary care indicate a need to treat the referring agents, such as general practitioners, as clients needing interventions – in this instance education about the referral process and the nature of problems relevant for help with CBT. Given the alternative of doing nothing, this seems the most appropriate and ethical option. Any attempt to reduce referral baggage, whether of etiquette, misinformation or other negative experience, is to be applauded.

ACTIVITY **3.1**

Imagine you approached your general practitioner for help with a mental health difficulty and, with your agreement, you were referred to a CB practitioner. It is the morning of your first appointment. Imagine what you might feel, the thoughts that might be going through your head. What specific things might you be worried about? What would you want from that first session? How would you expect or want your CB therapist to behave? What would you expect from their style of dress? Their demeanour? Their questioning style?

Referral from, or related to, in-patient services

The referral baggage, described above in the context of clients in primary care, is often compounded in the experiences of clients who have experienced in-patient treatment. In the author's experience, it seems to be the rule rather than the exception that in-patient clients report negative experiences with a range of mental health workers, particularly the large numbers of junior medical staff that they see and who confer on them a range of, often confusing and conflicting, diagnostic labels. In such circumstances, CB therapists often have to spend several sessions debriefing clients before CBT assessment can begin. In these debriefing sessions, clients often describe breaches of standards of basic etiquette that should form the basis of positive encounters with mental health workers. These will be described immediately below, when poor practice will indicate some obvious standards of good practice for first and subsequent encounters.

The first encounter

Clearly, the first encounter influences the client's expectations of what and what not to expect from CBT. Sadly, it is often the case that deviant etiquette norms of mental health generally are transported into CBT practice. These are punctuality breaches (the CBT therapist not turning up on time for the first meeting with the client – being late without apologising for this); inappropriate dress that signals disrespect or a lack of concern for the client (scruffy clothes, such as worn jeans or old trainers); the display of boundary problems from the outset in the use of inappropriate language terms to address the client, often signalling over-familiarity (using the client's Christian name without asking if this is acceptable to them), or over-general 'street' terms used to address the client (for example 'mate' or 'love'); seeing clients in an environment which is inappropriate to conduct an assessment in (such as an untidy room which is normally used to store furniture).

REFLECTION POINT

Imagine that you are a client and that your first encounter with your CBT therapist was that they:

- turned up half an hour late for their appointment with you and, acting as if nothing was amiss, failed to apologise to you;
- are dressed in a torn T-shirt, old, worn trainers, torn jeans and have greasy, uncombed hair;
- call you 'love' or 'mate' – this may depend on your gender, although they may call you 'mate' if you are a woman;
- take you to an old, cold room, with hard chairs and no decorative items, such as wall hangings or flowers.

How would you feel:

- during the session?
- after the session?

All the above has happened and will continue to happen. So, quite clearly, mental health workers new to the practice of CBT should be mindful of the above and ensure that first and subsequent encounters with clients are characterised by punctuality, and appropriateness of dress, demeanour, language, assessment and treatment environment.

RESEARCH SUMMARY

Centrally important in the collaborative enterprise that characterises contemporary CBT assessment is the personal meaning-making of the client and the need for the therapies to adapt to this. The therapist takes the position that the focus is both at the phenomenological level, the client's inner life world . . . and of equal importance is the client's perception and experiences of the external world, such as conflicts at home, within relationships, experiences at work, and the coping behaviours used in these contexts.

(Grant, et al., 2008, p2)

The rudiments of assessment

The processes of case formulation development and assessment are interlinked in CB practice (Grant, et al., 2008). However, a comprehensive assessment is necessary to begin to develop a good, working case formulation. The main aims of assessment are to:

- find out what the client's problems are in clear, specific and measurable terms;
- identify the factors that serve to maintain both the problem, or problems, and the client's vulnerability to such problems;
- determine the impact of the problem, or problems, on the client's life;
- construct a continually developing case formulation;
- establish a baseline against which to evaluate the progress and success of the CB intervention.

All the above aims are inter-related, in that fulfilling one will help fulfil the others. To illustrate this, let's look in detail at each in turn, with a hypothetical client in mind.

Find out what the client's problems are in clear, specific and measurable terms

What does this mean? Well, clients often express their problems in very vague and non-specific terms. Someone with agoraphobic problems may, for example, say 'I just seem to have problems getting out'. To aim for clarity and specificity, the CB therapist would do well to ask this client 'Okay. So what can't you do exactly that you used to be able to do?' The client might reply 'Oh, you know, I can't go to Tesco, my local supermarket, any more to get my shopping.'

The therapist, and the client, now have achieved more problem-specificity. However, the therapist needs to validate the client, while finding out what other specific things they are unable to do and state these in measurable ways. 'Okay, that must be really restricting for you. I wonder if there's anything else that you can't do that illustrates your problem, or, to put it another way, that you would be doing if you didn't have your difficulties?' In response to this question, the client might give a list of things that they currently cannot do, such as go to their local gym, have nights out with friends, or walk down busy streets.

After having established exactly how often the client would go to the above places, the CB therapist and the client have achieved the aim of finding out the client's problems in clear, specific and measurable ways. They can then make the following list:

- Unable to go to Tesco, once a week, spending approximately one hour there.

- Unable to attend my local gym, three times a week, for one and a half hours each time.

- Unable to go to restaurants or my local pub, on a once weekly basis, for about three hours each time.

Identify the factors that serve to maintain both the problem, or problems, and the client's vulnerability to such problems

On further exploration, our client might reveal maintaining factors for both his current problems and for future vulnerability. The dialogue between the therapist and client might go something like this:

Therapist: What is it, do you think, that stops you going to Tesco, the gym and out with friends? Can you see any common factor?

Client: Well, I'm just really scared of these things. When I think of them I start to feel anxious and scared.

Therapist: Okay, I can see that must be really frightening for you. However, I wonder if we can just bear with this issue for a little while longer? Yes? Okay, I wonder if I can ask you to close your eyes and imagine going to Tesco after this session. This is hypothetical. I'm not going to ask you to do it . . . Okay? Can you do this and tell me how it makes you feel in your body and what kinds of thoughts go through your mind about it?

Client: Doing that makes me feel really panicky and faint, and I have images in my head of passing out in Tesco or making a fool of myself, by fainting or something.

Therapist: Okay, you've done well to engage with this exercise. Thank you. I think it's giving us really important information about your problem and what's maintaining it.

Client: How so?

Therapist: Well let's start with your problem first. Just thinking about the busy public situations that you've identified results in you feeling physical sensations of anxiety and having thoughts and images of bad things happening when you're in them.

Client: Y . . . es . . . I guess so.

Therapist: And that being the case, I guess it makes perfect sense to you to avoid getting into those situations in the first place?

Client: Yes, that's right. You've got it in one.

Therapist: Okay, if we can broaden out from your current difficulties and consider the following: many people have learned to use avoidance as a coping strategy to deal with threatening situations, or challenges, throughout their lives. I wonder if you could just have a think about that proposition for a moment and consider the extent to which it's true for you in any way?

Client: Yes, I guess that I've always tended to be a bit avoidant. When I look back at my life . . . my mother never encouraged us to be adventurous, and she was timid herself, so I've kind of grown up to avoid life's challenges. I very much regret that . . . I think I could have done much more with my life, potentially, than I have up to now.

Determine the impact of the problem, or problems, on the client's life

At this stage in the assessment process, it is becoming clear that, in keeping with people with anxiety disorders generally, and people with phobic anxiety specifically, avoidance is a major factor in maintaining their current phobic anxiety. In broader terms, in terms of life goals, avoidance is also serving to keep the client from finding out just what could be achieved in their life if they responded to life's challenges rather than shying away from them.

Given the above, it may be useful at this stage for the therapist and client to prioritise the problems before talking about their impact. The dialogue might go something like this:

Therapist: Okay, if I can just summarise what we've arrived at so far, it seems that you have both immediate and broad, long-standing, life problems, but they're both connected by the strategy of avoidance? The immediate problems are what we describe as 'agoraphobic'. You have difficulty getting into specific types of busy social situations where you fear you might pass out and/or make a fool of yourself. You might want to call that social failing? On the larger front, because of key messages you've received while growing up, you avoid challenges because of the fear of social failure?

Client: Wow, yes. I can see how the immediate and bigger problems hang together now, by the same theme.

Therapist: Good. It sounds like that's a bit of a relief for you? Would it be useful, do you think, for us to focus and work on the immediate agoraphobic problems first, then the broader life issues?

Client: Yes, that makes sense.

Therapist: Okay, let's have a think about how the agoraphobic problems and the broader life issues interfere with your life. We've already talked about what the agoraphobic difficulties stop you doing and how the broader avoidance pattern has kept you from achieving according to your abilities, or indeed finding out exactly what your abilities might be.

Client: Yes, that's right.

Therapist: Okay. Now, a useful strategy, and one which may help us a lot later on when we begin to hopefully see improvement with your difficulties, is to give a numerical rating to each problem area with regard to how much it negatively interferes with your life. Have a look at this scale:

0		2	4		6	8
no interference		slight	moderate		great	maximum interference

Now, thinking about your agoraphobic problems generally, where would you put yourself on this scale in terms of how much you think they interfere with your life?'

Client: Well, at the moment, I'd say maximum . . . 8.

Therapist: And what about the problem of avoiding life challenges? How much does that interfere?

Client: Oh, I guess between 4 and 6, maybe 5.

Construct a continually developing case formulation

At this point, the therapist and client are in a position to begin the process of constructing a case formulation. This is helpful in that it enables the client to consolidate their progress so far and understand how the various aspects of their difficulties hang together. Based on the above dialogue between therapist and client, the formulation will be in two parts as shown in Figures 3.1 and 3.2.

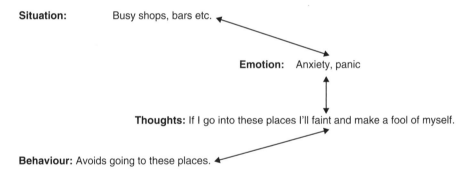

Figure 3.1 Agoraphobic formulation

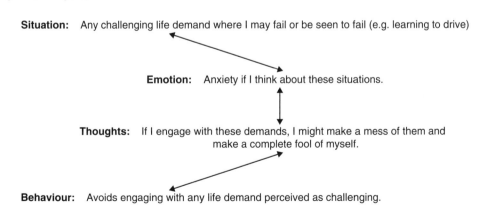

Figure 3.2 Broader life problems formulation

Establish a baseline against which to evaluate the progress and success of the CB intervention

The client and therapist already have baseline measures for the two problem areas. The measures are 8 for the agoraphobic problems and 5 for the life challenges. However, similar to map reading, these measures should be seen as a reference point for where the client is now. Reference points still need to be taken for where the client is headed (often described as the client's goals), as the following brief section of dialogue will illustrate.

Therapist: Okay, focusing on your agoraphobic problems for the moment, let's imagine four months have elapsed and you are no longer afraid of shops, bars and so on. What would you be doing specifically that you're not doing now?

Client: Well, I'd be going to the supermarket as usual, once a week; to the gym three times a week and meeting my friends in social situations, in the evenings, about once a week.

Therapist: Okay, how about we write this down and keep these as our goals?

Client: Yes, good, but what about the other problem area?

Therapist: Yes, of course. Are there any life challenges that we could write down for you to engage in, hopefully after you've successfully tackled your first set of difficulties?

Client: Well, yes. Our discussion has got me thinking. I really should . . . would like to learn to drive. It's something that I've been putting off for years, but it would open up so many avenues for me.

Therapist: Yes, that sounds really positive. Let's write it down.

Assessment is a process, not a single event

The above represents what might take place during the early stages of assessment. It is really important to stress, however, that assessment should be seen as a *process* rather than an *event*. In reality, assessment never stops throughout the course of therapy. However, in an important sense, there is a beginning, middle and end to it. Therapy cannot begin proper until a case formulation, including problem and goal identification, has been developed. The (middle) work of CBT depends on having the formulation as a reference point, and ending therapy usually happens on the basis of the client's goal attainment.

C H A P T E R   S U M M A R Y

The process of preparing a client for CBT will vary according to clients' social contexts. It is vitally important for CBT referrals to be made on the basis of informed consent. This may take the form of verbal and written information about the CBT approach, and time for the client to think about a referral, if appropriate. Referral letters should contain helpful and accurate information. However, the referral process is often mismanaged on the basis of breaches of referral etiquette and referral misinformation. If this happens on a regular basis, referring agents may need education about the referral process. Clients from in-patient services may need extended debriefing because of their negative experiences.

The client's first encounter with CBT is vitally important, around norms of etiquette, punctuality, dress, boundaries, demeanour and environment.

If the rudiments of assessment are observed, this will enable the development of clear, specific and measurable problems and goals and a case formulation for each client. Assessment should be viewed as a process rather than a discrete, single event.

FURTHER READING

Grant, A, Townend, M, Mills, J and Cockx, A (2008) *Assessment and case formulation in cognitive behavioural therapy.* London: Sage Publications Ltd.

This text is an in-depth exploration of the inter-related nature of assessment and case formulation. The emerging principles are applied to a range of client-centred case studies.

Chapter 4
Helping anxious people

Styliani Gkika

C H A P T E R A I M S

After reading this chapter you will be able to:

- have a deeper understanding of the cognitive behavioural models for anxiety disorders;

- comprehend, and develop cognitive behavioural case formulations for anxiety-related problems;

- consider a variety of cognitive and behavioural interventions for anxiety disorders;

- assess service users needs and your own ability to empathise with their problems.

Introduction

This chapter will discuss the cognitive and behavioural rationales for anxiety disorders. Anxiety problems, such as negative thinking, unpleasant bodily sensations and anxious predictions are very common. Most of us know how distressing and uncomfortable these can become. More extreme features of anxiety, but still quite common ones, are panic attacks and excessive worrying. Intense and prolonged anxiety is the main element of most anxiety disorders, which can severely interfere with the everyday life and mood of individuals.

In the following sections, we will explore some formulations of anxiety and their clinical implications. We will discuss assessment and interventions tailored to address anxiety problems, without discounting the importance of individual differences and cultural issues. Finally, we will focus on specific anxiety disorders from a cognitive behavioural perspective.

What is anxiety? Is anxiety a learned response to external or internal stimuli?

ACTIVITY 4.1

Using the internet and library resources, look up the stimulus–response theories proposed by Pavlov, Watson and Skinner. Try to identify what the theories are about and their similarities and differences.

> **REFLECTION POINT**
>
> *What do you notice about yourself and your surroundings when you feel anxious?*

Early learning theories (known from Pavlov and his experiments on dogs, and integrated into psychology by Watson) have proposed that stimulus–response interactions can explain anxiety. In particular, classical conditioning suggests that an unconditional stimulus, such as a thunderstorm occurring when someone's in a forest, can result in the response of fear. At the same time, other stimuli (the sound of thunder) can become conditioned to the same reaction (fear) as the unconditional stimulus (thunderstorm). Subsequently, the sound of thunder can be associated with fear even when we are safe at home.

Moreover, Skinner proposed that humans not only react to and learn from external stimuli but also have the ability to manipulate and learn from their responses and further experiences. He suggested, therefore, that there is an interaction between the Antecedent (the object, situation, and so on that initiates the response), the subsequent *Behaviour*, and the Consequences (this is sometime known as the A–B–C model). For example, if a boyfriend gives his girlfriend flowers and she responds with a kiss, then the boyfriend learns that this behaviour (offering flowers to my girlfriend) results in a reward (a kiss), and he is therefore likely to repeat the behaviour. Similarly, if someone has associated something (e.g. loud thunder) with a negative outcome (e.g. fear), then that person is likely to try a variety of strategies to reduce the fear. If increasing the volume of the TV (hence avoiding listening to the thunderstorm) reduces the fear (reward), then the behaviour is likely to be repeated.

Nevertheless, the above rationale fails to account for more complex expressions of anxiety, stress, and fear (such as being afraid of things that have never been associated with danger or threat), as well as for individual differences (why is it that some people who have experienced a traumatic experience do not go on to develop post-traumatic stress disorder?). A contemporary learning theory perspective, namely the Diathesis-Stress model, addresses the above criticisms.

The Diathesis-Stress model

The Diathesis-Stress model (see Mineka and Zinbarg, 2006 for a review) incorporates in its rationale three major factors:

1. Early learning histories and everyday life experiences that influence our vulnerability to events.

2. The extent to which these events are uncontrollable.

3. The life experiences (and 'lessons') that follow these events.

> **CASE STUDY**
>
> *Mary has a family history of anxiety disorders. In addition, her parents were over-protective and never reinforced her to explore new things or take any risks (vulnerability factors). When she was 12 years old, her parents had a big Christmas meal with relatives and friends. Mary got sick in front of everybody (uncontrolled situation). She felt very embarrassed (possible influence from social or interpersonal standards) and ran to her room. She felt humiliated and ashamed. Mary has been afraid of vomiting ever since. Amongst other activities, she has been avoiding eating in front of others, travelling with public transportation, and speaking about food (chained conditioning to several external stimuli). If she is asked to participate in any of these activities, she gets extremely anxious and terrified (conditioned response).*

Moreover, this model suggests that conditioning can occur from personal experiences as well as from observations, and from internal stimuli, such as increased heart rate conditioned with a panic attack, as well as from external stimuli such as exposure to spiders conditioned with a panic attack.

ACTIVITY 4.2

Can you think of examples of conditioning from your own experiences? Gather a few examples and then compare them in terms of vulnerability factors, uncontrollability and conditioning. Use Form 4.1 to help.

Is anxiety a response to the way we think?

A different rationale is offered by the cognitive theories that focus on thoughts and beliefs as factors that regulate emotion. For example, several authors have put particular emphasis on cognitive appraisals (Beck, 1976; Lazarus and Folkman, 1984; Ellis, et al., 2001). These authors have suggested that our emotional and behavioural responses are not linked directly to a given event; rather, they are linked to our interpretation of that event.

Beck and Emery (1985) suggested that cognitive, emotional and behavioural interactions maintain emotional disorders. This cognitive model focuses on the knowledge and the strategies that life experiences store in our long-term memory. This knowledge develops into a cognitive set of assumptions and rules for living (e.g. 'I must always smile and say hello to the people I like'). These assumptions, along with self-knowledge and self-beliefs (e.g. 'I am an interesting person'), form our self-schemas.

When we enter a threatening situation, we try to measure the threat and our coping strategies, and decide upon the level of our vulnerability (Beck and Emery, 1985). However, rigid and inflexible assumptions and rules can lead to negative appraisals, selective attention to the negative, negative automatic thoughts, negative feelings, and certain behavioural responses (fight, flight or freeze). Fixation into a certain belief system and a particular type of responding to threats develops into a dominant *mode* (e.g. the depressive mode, the hostile mode, and so on). This dominant mode can hold us trapped into vicious cycles of thoughts–feelings–behaviour interactions.

Appraisals that involve danger and threat are linked to fear; appraisals that involve violating personal rules are linked to anger; appraisals that involve violating personal standards are linked to shame; appraisals that involve responsibility for a negative outcome are linked to guilt; and appraisals that involve loss are linked to sadness (Beck, 1976).

In addition, people tend to seek the reasons for important events. Abramson, et al. (1978) have suggested that such cognitive attributions can be internal (e.g. 'it was my fault') or external (e.g. 'it was someone else's fault'), global (e.g. 'everything I do turns out badly') or specific (e.g. 'it only happened this once'), and stable (e.g. 'it's always like this') or unstable (e.g. 'it's a matter of chance'). The type of attribution given to an external or internal event influences the individual's emotional and behavioural response.

In brief, Clark and Beck (2009) formulate cognition in three basic stages (Figure 4.1):

1. The initial registration when we decide whether a situation/event is noxious or not. In this stage the schemas are activated and influence the next two stages.

2. The primal mode that is partly automatic and partly conscious. During this stage there is cognitive, emotional, and behavioural activation – for example, negative automatic thoughts occur.

3. The secondary elaboration when cognitive re-appraisal of the situation takes place (e.g. worry) and current schemas are activated.

Form 4.1

Crucial event	Response	Vulnerability factors	Uncontrollability of the event	Conditioned stimuli	Conditioned responses
E.g. Mary got sick at the family meal	E.g. she felt embarrassed, anxious, afraid, and ran to her room	E.g. she was never trusted to deal with new and risky situations. Possibly she had some genetic predisposition to anxiety. She might have developed a social norm against vomiting in public	E.g. she could not prevent being sick	E.g. she associated danger and fear with many food and travelling situations	E.g. when confronted with these situations she became extremely anxious
Write your examples here					

29

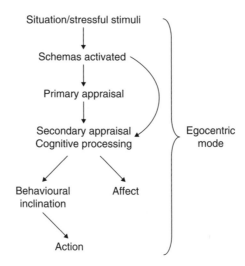

Figure 4.1 Links between cognitions and anxiety (affect) based on the cognitive model of anxiety (Clark and Beck, 2009)

Moreover, the above negative thoughts are linked to counter-productive coping strategies, such as avoidance and safety behaviours. Avoidance prevents us from testing whether our fear is as bad as we think it is, and whether we can cope with the situation or the negative emotion. Safety behaviours (Salkovskis, 1991) are the behaviours we employ to protect ourselves from negative outcomes (e.g. pretending to look for something in the handbag to avoid interaction, or sitting near the exit in a crowded restaurant). Safety behaviours do not allow us to disconfirm our maladaptive assumptions.

CASE STUDY

Some friends asked Mary to join them for dinner at their house. Mary immediately thought 'What if I get sick in front of them? That would be terrible. They will be disgusted and never want to be near me again. I will be left alone.' Cognitive therapists term these thoughts Negative Automatic Thoughts (NATs), because they are involuntary and intrusive. Such thoughts are likely to distress Mary (impact on feelings) to the point that she refuses to accept the invitation (impact on behaviour). Avoidance of the meal will prevent Mary from testing all these negative thoughts: will she be sick? Even if she is, will her friends reject her? Given that her worries and anxious predictions are not challenged or disconfirmed, her fear is likely to persist. The cognitive model suggests that it is the interpretation of a situation as potentially embarrassing that may result in anxiety, and not the situation itself. Therefore, certain beliefs (appraisals and rules) underlie the thoughts–feelings–behaviour cycle. Mary has assumptions such as 'If I am sick in front of people then everybody will hate me', 'If someone doesn't like me then there must be something wrong with me', 'I must never make someone upset.'

ACTIVITY 4.3

Go back to the examples you have written for the previous exercise. Can you remember what was going through your mind when you encountered the situations described? Can you remember how you felt and what you did? Were you following any rules or did you form any rules after these situations?

Is anxiety a response to the way we think about our own thinking?

The meta-cognitive model for emotional disorders (Wells, 2009) focuses on 'meta-cognition': meta-cognition refers to our understanding and experience of the ways in which our minds work (Grant, et al., 2010; Wells, 1997; Wells, 2002). The meta-cognitive model distinguishes between beliefs (e.g. 'If I show signs of anxiety, then people will think I am weak') and meta-cognitive beliefs (e.g. 'The fact that I think that "if I show any signs of anxiety, then people will think I am weak", means that I am weak'). Meta-cognitive beliefs are the beliefs we hold about our own thinking. Other examples are: 'If I worry too much, I will drive myself crazy'; 'If I am getting caught by my thoughts then I must be damaged'; 'If I have no control over my thoughts then my life will be destroyed'; 'Worrying will help me find a solution.' Meta-cognitive beliefs can be positive or negative. Negative meta-cognitive beliefs can refer to the dangerousness and uncontrollability of thoughts.

These types of belief are important because it is suggested that they regulate coping mechanisms and strategies that can influence emotional and behavioural responses (Wells and Matthews, 1994). For example, someone who believes firmly that worrying is a helpful strategy to use in problem solving is likely to worry extensively when faced with a problem. Nevertheless, if the problem has no immediate solution, then the person is likely to worry for a prolonged period of time, and worry is usually accompanied by unpleasant feelings. Negative beliefs about worry may interfere with someone's life experience (such as that worrying can drive someone mad or that it is uncontrollable), therefore increasing negative mood even more.

These meta-cognitive beliefs are verbal expressions of our meta-cognitive self-knowledge (knowledge of our cognitive functioning). The meta-cognitive beliefs regulate mechanisms such as worry, avoidance, safety-behaviours, rumination, self-focused attention and threat monitoring that form the Cognitive Attentional Syndrome.

Instead of targeting the dominant cognitive modes (Beck and Emery, 1985), the meta-cognitive model distinguishes between the *object* mode and the *meta-cognitive* mode (Wells and Matthews, 1994). The first enables us to respond to external information in a more or less involuntary and automatic way. The second enables us to process the information in a more conscious way. Therefore, the model targets information processing mechanisms, and the beliefs that regulate them.

In our example, Mary decided to reject her friend's invitation for dinner. She anticipated several negative scenarios and, reasonably, she decided to avoid them. What made Mary engage in this anticipatory thinking style? What made her worry in advance? Mary may believe that if she anticipates all possible negative outcomes, then she can be prepared, or perhaps she can protect herself. However, Mary may also believe that such anticipation will make her worked up and distressed. Mary's beliefs cause her to become trapped in a vicious cycle (worry–anxiety–avoidance), which is partly regulated by her positive and negative meta-cognitive beliefs for anticipatory thinking. The focus here is not so much on the content of her thoughts but rather on how these thoughts came about so intensely and persistently.

ACTIVITY **4.4**

Go back to your examples. Can you remember using any strategies, such as self-focused attention, threat monitoring, worry, or rumination? What are the advantages and disadvantages of using these strategies?

ACTIVITY **4.5**

Can you think of any pros and cons for each of the approaches discussed above? Which one(s) would you prefer to describe your experiences and why?

Assessment

Following our discussion so far, anxiety appears to have many complicated features. Thoughts, feelings, behaviours, belief systems and meta-cognition seem to be involved in its expression and maintenance. Therefore, assessment of anxiety involves assessment of its many characteristics.

Assessment is useful for understanding the individual's experience of anxiety, as well as for research. Therefore, a broad range of assessment tools has been developed. Antony, et al. (2001) have edited an informative book that lists most of the anxiety measures used today.

Frequently, clinicians assess anxiety with the help of self-report scales and questionnaires. These can target cognitions (e.g. beliefs, fears, and worries), somatic symptoms (e.g. tension, shaking, increased heart-rate), and behaviours (e.g. avoidance, safety behaviours, new skills). Some of the most commonly used questionnaires are:

- Beck's Anxiety Inventory (BAI) which is a 21-item measure of anxiety and the intensity of relevant bodily sensations (Beck, et al., 1988).

- The Depression Anxiety Stress Scales (DASS) which originally comprised 41 items, although a 21-item version of it is also available (Lovibond and Lovibond, 1995).

- The Meta-Cognitions Questionnaire (MCQ) which originally consisted of 65 items measuring the level of one's agreement with beliefs about worry and thought. Its shorter version (MCQ-30) comprises five sub-scales: positive beliefs about worry, negative beliefs about the uncontrollability and harmfulness of worry, beliefs about one's confidence of their cognitive functioning, beliefs about being aware of such cognitive functioning, and beliefs about the need to control thoughts (Wells and Cartwright-Hatton, 2004).

Other types of assessment are interviews (e.g. structured or unstructured questioning), scales (e.g. ranging from 0 to 100 or from 0 to 10), diaries, and thought records. The mental health worker's awareness of cultural issues and individual differences are crucial for clinical assessment and for the application of therapeutic interventions.

Cognitive behaviour therapy

Cognitive behaviour therapy (CBT) targets the thoughts, belief systems, and behaviours that keep the individual trapped in distressing emotional experiences. In particular, CBT aims to guide the individual to explore and challenge these beliefs. New, alternative and more flexible beliefs can replace the old ones. We refer to this procedure as *cognitive restructuring,* and we use several techniques to promote it.

Thought records and diaries

There is a great amount of literature that offers various examples and forms of thought records and diaries, most of them adapted for specific problems (Beck and Emery, 1985; Burns, 1990; Beck, 1995; Grant, et al., 2004; Greenberger and Padesky, 1995; Leahy, 2003; Leahy and Holland, 2000; Wells, 1997). For example, we can keep a record of the situations that trigger our anxiety during the week, the relevant thoughts, feelings and physical sensations, and the subsequent behaviours (including safety behaviours). In order to challenge a fear, we can collect the evidence that supports and the evidence that does not support the relevant anxious 'hot-thoughts' (Greenberger and Padesky, 1995) or anxious predictions (Fennell, 1999).

Ratings, in the form of a 0–100 percentage or a 0–10 scale rating, can also be used in order to clarify the intensity of the feelings occurring in different situations, the level of belief in a thought or assumption, and the level of belief in alternative assumptions.

Nevertheless, thought records and diaries can be very challenging. A common difficulty is that anxiety develops so fast that it is difficult to remember the thoughts and environmental factors that triggered it. Avoidance and safety behaviours can also prevent experiencing and exploring anxiety. Furthermore, there can be a difficulty in distinguishing between thoughts and feelings (e.g. we commonly use expressions such as 'I feel I shouldn't be doing this' even though this is more likely to be a thought). Moreover, focusing on such thoughts and feelings and writing them down might be anxiety provoking in itself. Finally, hopelessness is one more factor that can interfere with collecting evidence and trying to view things from alternative perspectives.

Working with the case formulation: Deconstructing and reconstructing

The case formulation is a map of the individual's problems and underlying factors (e.g. beliefs, unhelpful strategies, etc.) (Grant, et al., 2008). A diagrammatic case formulation and any diagrams of vicious cycles can also be valuable tools for some service users. Diagrams can increase awareness, help put things into perspective and facilitate access of information (Larkin and Simon, 1987). Deconstructive and reconstructive questioning can help service users to discover ways of breaking the vicious cycles that they are trapped in. For example, therapist and service user can explore the main problem, its maintaining factors and the strategies used, and consider how the service user would like things to be different. They can draw an alternative case formulation and agree to certain steps that lead towards that direction. Case formulations can have an active role in CBT, in terms of developing a shared understanding of service users' problems and in designing appropriate treatment plans (Grant, et al., 2008).

A useful tool is *Socratic questioning*. This is a type of indirect questioning that guides rather than suggests. Socrates was an ancient Greek philosopher who used this type of questioning to break a problem (or philosophical question) into a series of questions, the answers of which would be likely to lead to the solution of the problem (or the answer to the initial question).

While working with a case formulation, Socrates could have asked . . .

How does everything link together? What strategies are used to deal with the problem? How helpful or unhelpful are they? What would be the costs and benefits of dropping some of the safety behaviours? How would the service user like things to be different? What would they like changed? If they woke up tomorrow and they were magically immune to fear, how would the formulation be different? What would they be thinking and doing differently? What strategies would they be using?

Using problem-focused interventions

The books of Leahy and Holland (2000) and Leahy (2003) are great resources of interventions specifically designed to deal with certain cognitive and behavioural difficulties. For example, the cognitive distortions list shows us how our thoughts can sometimes be misleading rather than accurate; a cost and benefits form can be used in order to decide on the usefulness of the safety behaviours and so on.

Behavioural reattribution

Perhaps the most frequently used technique for helping people with increased levels of anxiety and panic attacks is exposure. The more we expose ourselves to the feared situations, the less we are afraid of them. Our bodies respond to a threatening situation with anxiety. The physical symptoms of anxiety (e.g. increased heart rate, hyperventilation, etc.) are regulated by our sympathetic system. This system increases the levels of adrenaline and cortisone in our bodies. It does that to help us be alert and vigilant, and therefore capable of a fast response to the threat (flight, fight, or freeze). The sympathetic system is doing this to ensure our survival and therefore its reaction is immediate. When our organism feels safe again, then the parasympathetic system will calm things down and help us return to a balanced state. The two systems are opposing and complemented.

To translate the above in terms of exposure, let's use Mary's example. Once Mary perceives a threat (e.g. 'It's very hot in here, my stomach feels weird, I might vomit') she becomes anxious almost immediately. Her body responds with unpleasant and distressing physical sensations (e.g. nausea, tremor) that make her feel weaker. Following that, she usually attempts 'flight': that is, in trying to escape the situation. Exposure aims to make our bodies 'get used' to the situation. If Mary stays in the situation long enough, her parasympathetic system will eventually feel safe enough to let anxiety drop and her vital functions will return to their normal condition. According to conditional learning, a more adaptive response (e.g. to stay and try to relax) will replace the learned response of fear and flight. The result of this procedure is beneficial and rewarding, therefore likely to be repeated.

The above explanation and therapeutic technique is well respected and broadly applied especially in behavioural approaches. However, in terms of the cognitive behavioural approach it seems to lack focus on the cognitive part. Foa and Kozak (1986) and Salkovskis (1991) have suggested that exposure is only effective if cognitive change occurs. Furthermore, Thorpe and Salkovskis (1995) found that the fear experienced in specific phobias is not only a physiological response; rather, certain beliefs and cognitions regulate and maintain our responses, especially those of disgust, harm and inability to cope. For example, Edwards and Salkovskis (2006) suggested that disgust does not enhance the fear, rather the fear enhances disgust.

One way of applying exposure while aiming for cognitive change is to conduct a behavioural experiment. Bennett-Levy, et al. (2004) have edited a well-informed guide to behavioural experiments: *Oxford Guide to Behavioural Experiments in Cognitive Therapy*. With behavioural experiments we act as if we were researchers. We form our hypotheses (predictions) and structure

---

CASE STUDY

Mary decided to conduct an experiment. The hypothesis was that if she stayed in the library for more than ten minutes she would be sick in front of all the people and humiliated. Her alternative hypothesis was that maybe her stomach was only responding to the heat and to anxiety, and that she might not be sick after all. She suggested that if she focused on the task at hand rather than on her bodily sensations, then maybe her anxiety would drop. The next step was to do the experiment and see what happens. Then she would bring the results to therapy, discuss them further, reflect on them and plan future experiments.

ways of testing them out. Then we conduct the experiment, observe the outcome and draw our conclusions as well as suggestions for the future (what we learned from our experiment).

A well-designed behavioural experiment can always teach us regardless of negative or positive results. An 'unsuccessful' experiment (one where things went wrong) can be very distressing and discouraging for the service user. Therefore, the therapist needs to emphasise that the purpose of the experiments is to learn.

The rest of the chapter will focus on the cognitive behavioural rationales for specific anxiety disorders. Try to see if you can find cues from the above perspectives.

ACTIVITY 4.6

Have you ever changed a strong opinion or belief about something? For example, a religious belief, a prejudice, an opinion about someone, a behaviour, a strategy that did not work for you, the way you study or the way you interact with people?

What made you change? How did you change? Did someone convince you to change? How? Did you find arguments to support your new belief, strategy and so on? Did you make the change instantly or did it take some time? Did you start acting according to your new belief, opinion, or strategy? If yes, then how was behaviour different? Did you challenge your old beliefs? Did you try any experiments?

The phobic individual

Even though specific phobias (or simple phobias) are quite common (it is very likely that you or someone you know suffers from a phobia), nevertheless they have been given little attention. Approximately 10 per cent to 11.3 per cent of the general population has some type of specific phobia. These phobias usually develop during childhood or in adolescence. However, phobias can also appear in older ages, for example after a traumatic experience (APA, 1994).

According to the Diagnostic and Statistical Manual for psychiatric disorders – DSM-IV (APA, 1994) – the diagnostic criteria for specific phobias involve a persistent fear in anticipation or in the presence of the feared object or situation, acute anxiety, and consequent avoidance of the feared object or situation. Phobic individuals acknowledge the fear as irrational or exaggerated. The diagnosis is given if the person experiences the condition for more than six months, and if the condition influences their everyday functioning (e.g. occupational, educational, social life) or mood. The symptoms should not be better explained by another disorder, such as panic disorder, obsessive compulsive disorder or social phobia (APA, 1994).

Furthermore, the DSM-IV (APA, 1994) categorises specific phobias into five sub-types:

- Situational Type (e.g. airplanes, driving, enclosed spaces)
- Natural Environment Type (e.g. thunderstorms, heights)
- Blood, Injection, Injury Type
- Animal Type (e.g. spiders, snakes)
- Other Type (e.g. situations that might lead to illness, choking, vomiting).

Cognitive behavioural conceptualisation for specific phobias

Kirk and Rouf (2004) have developed a comprehensive cognitive conceptualisation for specific phobia (Figure 4.2). According to their model, specific phobias can be influenced by several factors, such as biological predisposition, the person's developmental stage, cultural issues, previous relevant experiences, memories and beliefs. These factors lead to the adoption of certain assumptions or rules for living. For example, previous and scary experiences with heights may have led someone to develop the assumption that 'If I am anywhere high, I will feel anxious and lose control.'

Such assumptions increase a sense of vulnerability when faced with the feared situations and make people hyper-vigilant. Certain rules, such as 'I must never feel anxious', maintain the fear by regulating behaviour. Behavioural responses typically involve avoidance and safety behaviours as coping mechanisms. However, these mechanisms are counter-productive because they prevent facing the problem, experiencing and processing disconfirmatory information (i.e. information that suggests that the feared scenario might not actually happen), and confidence building.

The feared situation or object is likely to activate anxious thoughts and predictions (e.g. 'What if I lose control, fall, and die?' or 'What if someone pushes me?'). These anxious cognitions are generated by an overestimation of danger and an underestimation of coping strategies. This links to negative emotions, physiological reactions and unhelpful behaviours. The whole process leads to secondary problems, such as depression, hopelessness, loss of confidence and low self-esteem.

The model in Figure 4.2 illustrates the complexity of specific phobias. Several pieces of information need to be elicited to gain an understanding of the service user's personal experience. This information is elicited through questioning and questionnaires. In order to increase the element of self-exploration and discovery, Socratic questioning is preferred. That gives the service user the chance to make their observations and self-exploration and draw their own conclusions. Care is taken to check that the model fits the service user's experience and that no attempt is made to make the user's experiences fit the model. Service users might give emphasis to different aspects of the model and Socratic questioning enables us to 'follow' the service user's understanding of the situation and their resources, rather than 'lead' them towards the directions we would like (Padesky, 1993). After all, service users are the experts regarding their own experiences.

ACTIVITY 4.7

Think about a previous time when something scared you.

- *What triggered your fear? How did you feel? What did you notice happening in your body?*
- *Do you remember what was going through your mind during that time? What did you think of the situation? What did you think of your own response to the situation?*
- *What did you do? Did you do anything to protect yourself?*
- *What did you learn from your experience?*
- *How did your experience influence you in future situations?*

Socialisation and normalisation

One of the DSM-IV (APA, 1994) diagnostic criteria for specific phobias states that most phobic individuals know that their fear is unreasonable. Consider how you would feel if you believed that what you were doing made no sense to you or anybody else, yet you were unable to stop doing it.

CBT deals with that in a paradoxical way. On the one hand, challenging cognitions, working with cognitive distortions, and using behavioural experiments to disconfirm the fear are techniques that indicate that the given fear is indeed 'unreasonable' and therefore needs to be dealt with. On the other hand, an efficient and collaboratively developed case formulation aims to help us make sense of the individual's experience. If something makes sense, how can it be unreasonable?

REFLECTION POINT

- *Who decides what is reasonable or normal and what is not?*
- *How many people experience anxiety problems in their lifetime?*
- *Is being unreasonable the same as being inaccurate?*
- *Does an unreasonable fear belong to an unreasonable person?*

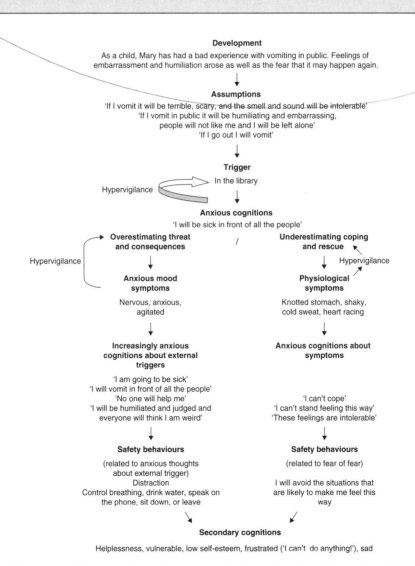

Figure 4.2 Detailed idiosyncratic case formulation for Mary based on Kirk and Rouf (2004, p163)

Educating service users about the model and collaboratively negotiating the treatment plan are crucial features of cognitive behaviour therapy. Normalisation though is also important given that it enables further exploration and understanding of the problem rather than just labelling people or reactions as abnormal or strange. Cultural issues also need to be addressed and individual differences should always be taken into account. The aim is not to prove all the negative thoughts and beliefs 'wrong'; the aim is to develop a more adaptive, flexible and balanced way of thinking that allows 'wrong' and 'right' thoughts to co-exist without causing too much trouble.

The individual with panic disorder

According to the DSM-IV (APA, 1994), a panic attack is an intense fear or discomfort linked to a series of physical symptoms that develop rapidly and arrive at their highest point within 10–20 minutes. Some of these physical symptoms are sweating, chest pain, dizziness and nausea. The diagnosis for panic disorder requires that the panic attacks are recurrent, and that the individual has been worried about further attacks and their consequences for a period of more than a month. Also, a significant behavioural change needs to take place. Often, but not always, agoraphobia accompanies panic disorder. Agoraphobia is an intense fear of places or situations where escape or help is difficult (e.g. crowded places, long queues and trains).

Cognitive behavioural conceptualisation for panic disorder

The cognitive behavioural model for panic disorder suggests that a panic attack develops when bodily sensations are misinterpreted as threatening (Clark, 1986). For example, increased heart rate can be interpreted as a sign of having a heart attack. The perceived danger leads to increased anxiety; anxiety regulates bodily sensations; bodily sensations confirm the fear that there is something physically wrong and that the catastrophe is about to happen. What can follow is a full-blown panic attack.

Goldstein and Chambless (1978) suggested the term 'fear of fear', meaning that people with panic disorder fear the sensations that accompany fear and therefore they avoid situations that may provoke them. In addition, these authors proposed that negative beliefs about the consequences of anxiety play an important role in the regulation of 'fear of fear'. Chambless, et al. (2000) also found four broad categories of symptoms that can set off 'fear of fear': cardiovascular, neurological, gastrointestinal (e.g. 'I feel nauseous, I am going to be sick') and behavioural (e.g. 'I am losing control; I will go insane and start behaving weirdly'). Apart from 'fear of fear', catastrophic misinterpretations may include the element of humiliation or embarrassment (e.g. 'If I have a panic attack in public, people will think I am strange', 'People will laugh at me'). Relevant images may accompany these beliefs.

Reasonably, people who have experienced such intense fear become vigilant of signs that can indicate to them that the catastrophe is about to happen. Therefore, they may develop a heightened self-focus (Goldstein and Chambless, 1978; Wells, 1997) which allows them to monitor every bodily sensation they are experiencing and especially the ones relevant to their fears.

The human body responds to both internal and external stimuli. For example, our bodies are bound to respond to heat, cold, noise and so on as well as to distressing thoughts. In panic disorder, these bodily responses are perceived as signs that a catastrophe is about to happen. Consequently, the people who interpret bodily sensations as threatening need to take action to protect themselves. Such actions are safety-seeking behaviours and include leaning or sitting down when in fear of fainting, hyperventilating when in fear of suffocating, and avoiding any situation that can provoke the feared bodily sensations in the case of agoraphobia.

According to the DSM-IV (APA, 1994) and the NICE (2008) guidelines, the service user needs to be seen by a physician and appropriate tests should be taken to exclude physical conditions that can induce bodily sensations similar to those experienced in anxiety and panic. For example, interpreting increased heart rate as threatening would not be a misinterpretation in the case of someone with high blood pressure who has forgotten to take their pills.

The above suggestions are integrated in the diagrammatic case formulation of panic disorder in Figure 4.3.

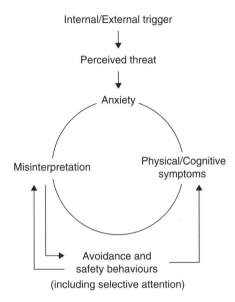

Figure 4.3 Cognitive model of panic (Clark, 1986) with maintenance cycles added (Wells, 1997)

Verbal reattribution for panic disorder

Verbal reattribution for panic disorder focuses mainly on challenging catastrophic misinterpretations. Initially, the aim is to normalise the experience, in order to illustrate that anyone facing such an intense danger would react with increased anxiety and would be likely to take action towards survival or safety (Casey, et al., 2004).

In addition, Wells (1997) suggests the use of metaphors and allegories in order to socialise the service users in the formulation's rationale and treatment plan. One example is the 'vampires' metaphor': some people believe in vampires and consequently they are afraid when in situations that vampires are known to appear (e.g. in the dark). In order to protect themselves they take precautions, such as wearing cloves of garlic around their necks or holding crucifixes. They may assume that the fact that they have never seen a vampire means that their precautions are working. How can these people discover that there are no vampires?

Behavioural reattribution for panic disorder

Behavioural experiments target three main elements: avoidance, escape and safety behaviours (Salkovskis, 2007). Furthermore, misinterpretations of danger are tested out as well as the service user's doubts about their own ability to cope with a distressing or emergency situation (Hackmann, 2004).

The best way to move towards designing a behavioural experiment is to form 'if . . . then' statements because they can be specific and testable. For example, think of the difference between the statement 'I am afraid of going out and I do not like crowded places at all' and the statement 'If I go out and there are people around, I will have a panic attack. People will see me and think that I am mad.' Which statement is easier to test?

Clinical improvement will be greatest if behavioural experiments offer as many opportunities for disconfirmation of the feared catastrophes as possible (Salkovskis, et al., 2007).

RESEARCH SUMMARY

Salkovskis and his colleagues (Salkovskis, et al., 2007) conducted an experiment to explore whether belief disconfirmation plays a role in the outcome of exposure therapy. Sixteen patients with panic disorder and agoraphobia participated in the study. All participants had a few initial sessions that included education about habituation, belief disconfirmation and dropping safety behaviours. Then, half received habituation exposure therapy and half received CBT exposure therapy (including belief disconfirmation and dropping of safety behaviours). To measure the outcome of therapy, participants were asked to take a 'behavioural walk'. They had to walk to their car, drive to the centre of the town, get out of the car and walk to a lamppost visible from the car, reach a square at the end of the street, go to a crowded pedestrian precinct, walk through a mall, go to the bus stop and take the bus back to the starting point. Both habituation exposure and CBT exposure proved helpful. Nevertheless, CBT exposure was associated with greater improvement in anxiety, self-reported agoraphobia, agoraphobic cognitions and the frequency of panic attacks. Furthermore, participants in the CBT exposure condition achieved more tasks at the behavioural walk and experienced less peak anxiety during the 'walk' than participants in the habituation exposure condition.

The individual with health anxiety

Health anxiety (or hypochondriasis) involves extreme preoccupation with the possibility of having a severe physical illness. Individuals with health anxiety misinterpret bodily sensations as signs of serious or lethal diseases. Such interpretation causes great distress and can influence the individual's everyday functioning. Diagnosis requires that this preoccupation does not subside when appropriate tests and physicians have ruled out any actual health problems, and that it lasts for more than six months (APA, 1994). Furthermore, the DSM-IV (APA, 1994) requires clinicians to specify if there is poor insight: meaning that the individuals do not acknowledge the possibility that the fear can be exaggerated or unreasonable. Health anxiety is classified as a somatoform disorder (APA, 1994).

Cognitive behavioural conceptualisation for health anxiety

The cognitive behaviour model for health anxiety is very similar to that for panic disorder. The health-anxious individual interprets bodily sensations as signs of a severe or lethal illness. The difference is that in panic disorder the individual believes that the catastrophe is happening here and now, whereas in health anxiety the individual believes that the catastrophe is going to happen in the near or distant future (e.g. 'This could be a symptom of cancer; what if I have cancer?'). Reasonably, many people with health anxiety visit their physicians frequently in order to check their health status. However, others prefer not to have contact with physicians, hospitals and other situations that can trigger their worries. In addition, health-anxious individuals tend to use a variety of safety behaviours in order to ensure that they limit the risk of illness. They engage in increased checking, avoidance and reassurance seeking. Self-focused attention is usually dominant (focusing on bodily sensations, especially the ones related to the specific illnesses they worry about). Furthermore, Wells (1997) reports 'selective abstraction', meaning that people tend to focus on the bits of information that confirm their misinterpretations while discounting the information that disconfirms it.

Salkovskis (1989), and Warwick and Salkovskis (1990) have formed a cognitive behavioural formulation for health anxiety: the disorder is strongly linked to previous experiences – for example, of a friend or relative who died of an illness. These previous experiences have led to the development of dysfunctional schemas that regulate the fear. A 'critical incident' or a bodily sensation in the person's everyday life triggers these schemas and activates negative automatic thoughts. A series of cognitive, emotional and behavioural responses follow (Figure 4.4).

CASE STUDY

Gus decided to test out the hypothesis: 'If I have a panic attack in the middle of the street, people will think I am mad.' He prepared a questionnaire with questions such as 'What would you think about a person who is walking near you in the street and suddenly stops, goes pale, starts shaking and leaves from the opposite direction?' and 'What would you do if someone fainted in front of you in the street?' He administered the questionnaire to friends and colleagues and discovered that most people would think that the person felt fatigued or tired or had forgotten something and had to go back and get it. In the case of fainting, most people would be concerned and try to help or ignore it if the person was already being helped. The results created doubt enough to motivate the service user to start going out.

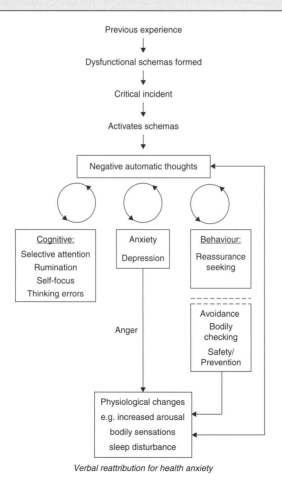

Verbal reattribution for health anxiety

Figure 4.4 A diagrammatic formulation of the cognitive model for health anxiety (Salkovskis, 1989; Warwick and Salkovskis, 1990) by Wells (1997)

Verbal reattribution for health anxiety

In health anxiety, guided discovery is very important because it can help service users to discover and formulate an idiosyncratic case formulation that makes sense to them: that is, one that explains their symptoms better than the possibility of having a physical illness. Wells (1997) suggests a series of socialisation experiments, including keeping a diary of the physical symptoms. Such a diary can lead to the discovery of specific patterns (for example, if specific symptoms occur at specific times, and if there is a connection between the symptom and the time or situation that it occurs in).

In health anxiety, challenging cognitive distortions and misinterpretations as well as meta-cognitions (worrying about worrying) – for example, 'If I continue worrying like this, I will go mad' – can be very useful. Health anxiety-specific meta-worries can mainly be about the loss of control over hypochondriac worries.

Educating the service user

Offering information about what can actually cause the feared physical illnesses can be useful, in order to weaken dysfunctional beliefs. For example, accurate information about the causes of fainting, strokes, heart attacks and so on can contradict the service user's beliefs that their particular physical symptoms indicate such conditions. Nevertheless, such information is not always available.

Furthermore, Wells (1997) suggests that certain beliefs and assumptions about death may play an important part in the maintenance of the vicious cycles. Therefore, they may need to be addressed and challenged to facilitate improvement and discharge the worrying that derives from enhanced emotions. Imagery can be very important since health-anxious individuals often have images of themselves having a lethal disease or dying.

Behavioural reattribution for health anxiety

Following the case formulation, behavioural experiments help challenge assumptions, worries, misinterpretations and dysfunctional coping strategies. Some examples follow.

- *The 'if . . . thens' that regulate worrying.* For example, 'If I worry about it, then I can be prepared in case the worse happens'; 'If I worry about it, then I can be vigilant and spot premature signs of the illness.'

- *The 'if . . . thens' that regulate behaviours.* For example, 'If I check, I will know if there is something wrong with me or not'; 'If I ask for reassurance, I will be relieved from worrying'; 'If I do not ask for reassurance, worrying will drive me crazy'; 'If I do not go to the physician, I will go undiagnosed and die a terrible death'; 'If I sense something weird and I do not know which illness's symptom it can be, then I will not know how to protect myself.'

- *The 'if . . . thens' that regulate misinterpretations.* For example, 'If I sense something in my head then maybe I have a brain tumour'; 'If I miss a heart-beat then I may be having serious heart problems'; 'If I get anxious all the time then too much adrenaline is going to cause damage in my body'; 'If there is a physical sensation then it must be signalling health problems'.

- *The 'if . . . thens' that regulate cognitions and images.* For example, 'If I think it, then it must be true'; 'If I can imagine it and it makes me scared, then it must be real.'

Silver, et al. (2004) offer ideas about behavioural experiments concerning three different categories of beliefs: (a) beliefs about the need to be responsible which maintain preoccupation and worry, (b) beliefs about health, illness and death and (c) beliefs about the effect of anxiety and worry.

> ### Socrates could have asked . . .
>
> *How likely would you be to go and visit the physician if you were experiencing minor flu symptoms and:*
>
> - *you were 100 per cent sure that they were the symptoms of meningitis?*
> - *you were 80 per cent sure that they were the symptoms of meningitis?*
> - *you were 60 per cent sure that they were the symptoms of meningitis?*
> - *you were 40 per cent sure that they were the symptoms of meningitis?*
> - *you were 20 per cent sure that they were the symptoms of meningitis?*
> - *you were 100 per cent sure that they were the symptoms of a cold?*

Excluding physical illnesses

The therapist needs to be cautious regarding the service user's physical symptoms. Thorough medical examinations can exclude health conditions that could induce the symptoms that the service users are experiencing. If the service user has been too afraid to undertake the necessary exams, then the therapist needs to initially work towards that direction. Psychotherapists are not physicians and therefore the symptoms need to be carefully explored before jumping into the conclusion that it is *only* anxiety that is causing the problem.

Nevertheless, therapists should be careful not to engage in service users' worries and ruminations. If the medical examination has been negative, then that can strengthen the formulation's rationale.

ACTIVITY *4.8*

Make two lists of the symptoms you experience when ill or tired and of the symptoms you experience when anxious or worried. What helps you distinguish between the two (e.g. experiences, knowledge, beliefs, sayings, friends etc.)?

The individual with obsessive compulsive disorder (OCD)

The diagnosis of OCD requires the experience of obsessions or compulsions that are time consuming, or interfere with the individual's everyday life functioning and mood. Nevertheless, the individual must acknowledge that these obsessions and compulsions are unreasonable (APA, 1994). The DSM-IV (APA, 1994) describes obsessions as recurrent and persistent thoughts, impulses, or images that are intrusive and cause distress, but are distinguished from worry-like thinking patterns. The individual will attempt to ignore or suppress such intrusions and will consider them unreasonable and distressing. Compulsions are repetitive behaviours (rituals) or mental acts (e.g. neutralising – for example, focusing on a very positive image to 'disarm' an intrusive negative one). Such compulsions offer some relief, however irrelevant they may appear.

Cognitive behavioural conceptualisation for OCD

Rachman and de Silva (1978) studied the occurrence and nature of intrusions in a clinical and non-clinical sample. Briefly, they found that about 80 per cent of the non-clinical participants experienced obsessions, and therefore suggested that obsessions are a common experience. They also found that these obsessions were similar for both clinical and non-clinical samples in terms of content, meaningfulness, form and expressed mood. They were different in terms of how long they lasted, how frequently they occurred, how intense they were and how much discomfort they caused.

This finding offered support to the assumption that intrusive thoughts are normal mental events. For example, an intrusion such as 'What if my friend died?' could be an ordinary (however unpleasant) mental event. Many people would be able to dismiss it as false and unimportant, unless there is proof to think otherwise (e.g. if the friend's life is indeed threatened).

However, in OCD the same intrusion could be appraised as valid and therefore extremely scary and distressing (e.g. 'Having a thought like that means that it is likely to happen' and therefore 'I must take action to prevent this from happening'). These type of appraisals are regulated by more general underlying assumptions, such as 'If I think about something bad happening and I don't take action to prevent it, then I am responsible for it if it happens' (Obsessive Compulsive Cognitions Working Group, 1997). Consequently, actions, such as constant checking, neutralising and safety behaviours, are applied to prevent the given catastrophe and to reduce distress. These behaviours are counterproductive and maintain the problem because they prevent the individual from discovering that the intrusion was just a thought rather than an actual fact. In other words, behaviours such as these prevent disconfirmation of negative appraisals and rigid assumptions (Salkovskis, 1991, 2004).

Cognitive therapy has placed great emphasis on the assumptions and appraisals implicated to OCD. According to the most commonly used cognitive model for OCD (Salkovskis, 1985; Salkovskis and McGuire, 2003) there seems to be a combination of appraisals of increased risk, and responsibility for either harming or for preventing harm from happening. These appraisals are characterised by great discomfort, self-focused attention towards the intrusions and environmental triggers, preoccupation with them and overt and/or covert responses (Salkovskis and McGuire, 2003), thus, leading to the formulation shown in Figure 4.5.

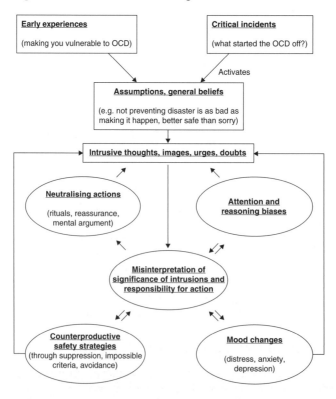

Figure 4.5 The cognitive model for OCD (Salkovskis and McGuire, 2003)

Early experiences are crucial in understanding vulnerability to OCD, as well as in exploring the onset of assumptions and appraisals. These assumptions are linked to intrusions, and then a series of vicious cycles begins. For example, attentional bias (increased focus on intrusions) makes intrusions more salient and likely to reappear, while feeding back to negative appraisals.

But how do people with OCD know when to stop their response behaviours? It is suggested (Salkovskis and McGuire, 2003) that while initially external criteria can be sufficient stop signals (e.g. ensuring that the door is locked), gradually internal criteria become more important (e.g. having a 'felt sense' that the ritual is complete).

Cognitive restructuring for OCD

The main belief systems addressed for further exploration and challenging shape the following categories (Obsessive Compulsive Cognitions Working Group, 1997):

- Inflated responsibility, as illustrated above.

- Over-importance of thoughts – for example, beliefs that some thoughts make the catastrophe more likely to happen and beliefs that having such thoughts characterise the individual as a person (e.g. 'Thinking about harming my children means I am evil'). The former is termed *likelihood thought action fusion* and the latter, *moral thought action fusion* (Shafran, et al., 1996).

- Beliefs about the controllability of thoughts – these are meta-cognitive beliefs because they are beliefs about thinking (e.g. 'If I can't control my thoughts, then I am going to go mad'; 'My intrusions are dangerous and uncontrollable') (Wells, 1997).

- Overestimation of threat – beliefs about exaggerated outcomes (e.g. 'If this happens, then it would be a disaster').

- Intolerance of uncertainty – beliefs about uncertainty, and an exaggerated need for certainty that make decision making difficult and confusing and reassurance seeking more likely (e.g. 'If I don't check, I will not know if the door is locked').

- Perfectionism.

- Fixated beliefs – rigid and inflexible beliefs.

Normalisation

Normalising includes informing service users about the nature of intrusive thoughts (Marks, 2003) and educating them about findings such as that about 80 per cent of the general population experiences thoughts similar in content and nature as theirs (Rachman and de Silva, 1978). Normalising is very important as it is the first step towards conceptualising the problem as one of thinking rather than one of actual threatening situations.

> **RESEARCH SUMMARY**
>
> *Purdon and Clark (1993) recruited 293 students to explore the nature of non-clinical obsessive thoughts. They administered a series of questionnaires about obsessive intrusions, anxiety, depression and general negative thinking. Women reported an average of seven intrusions, while men an average of eight. Men reported more intrusions under themes of sexual and aggressive behaviours, while women reported more intrusions about dirt and contamination. The most frequently mentioned intrusions were about causing harm or insulting friends, family, or strangers, reckless driving, impulsive sexual behaviour and catching sexually transmitted diseases, and leaving the house unlocked and being intruded. The dirt, sex and aggression groups of intrusions were linked to anxiety, depression and obsessive symptoms.*

Behavioural reattribution for OCD

Behavioural experiments are used in order to challenge appraisals, beliefs and behavioural responses, such as neutralising, thought suppression and rituals. Furthermore, behavioural experiments serve to test alternative and more adaptive beliefs and behavioural responses. Moreover, they can be a valuable tool in order to shift attention from negatively appraising intrusions and environmental triggers towards disconfirmatory information.

Exposure and response prevention (ERP)

Exposure and response prevention is an intervention that derived from behavioural models for OCD. The service user and the therapist create a hierarchical list of situations, things or thoughts avoided and agree on exposure tasks. These tasks can take place in-session or they can be in-vivo (in real life). Exposure is likely to trigger intrusions and negative appraisals and therefore response prevention is important. The individual is exposed to the feared situations (therefore tackling avoidance and safety behaviours), and with response prevention the person inhibits (does not follow through with) rituals and neutralisation. Therefore, the service user learns how to deal with feared situations in more adaptive ways.

In cognitive behavioural models, ERP is also employed in order to challenge maladaptive beliefs and appraisals. Exposure enables the individual to challenge beliefs and response prevention acts as a 'disconfirmatory manoeuvre' (Wells, 1997, p258) – that is, a way of directing thinking towards information that disconfirms the belief that a catastrophe will occur because of the intrusive thought.

The individual with post-traumatic stress disorder (PTSD)

The DSM-IV (APA, 1994) considers an experience to be traumatic if it involves actual or threatened death or severe injury of the self or others. Such experience invokes intense fear, a sense of helplessness, and horror. Not everyone who has experienced traumas will go on to develop PTSD. People are diagnosed with PTSD if they:

- have recurrent and intrusive memories of the event that cause them distress;
- experience distressing dreams that disturb their sleep;

- 'relive' the trauma as if it were happening here and now rather than as a past experience;

- experience acute distress and anxiety when exposed to cues that are linked to the trauma.

These symptoms should persist for more than a month, and should include avoidance (of thoughts, people, situations, etc.). Finally, PTSD can be acute (if its duration is less than three months), chronic (if its duration is more than three months), or with delayed onset, if the symptoms occur at least six months after the trauma (APA, 1994).

Cognitive behavioural conceptualisation for PTSD

Learning theorists attempted to develop an understanding of PTSD. Focusing on Mowrer's (1960) two-factor learning theory, behaviourists proposed that PTSD develops when the stimuli that were present during the trauma become conditioned with the emotional response of fear and distress. Then, chained conditioning occurs between superficially neutral stimuli and the emotional response. For example, sounds or voices that occurred at the same time as the trauma become associated with fear and distress. Therefore, similar sounds and voices can invoke these emotions even in situations irrelevant to the trauma situations. During these experiences of reliving the fear, even more stimuli can become conditioned to the same emotional response. Thus, the individual experiences uncontrollable emotional outbursts. The usual way out of these situations is through avoidance.

Cognitive theories take the discussion a step further by incorporating into the understanding of PTSD the role of cognitive appraisals (see Foa and Steketee, 1989). These theorists suggest that the traumatic experience links to more severe PTSD symptoms if individuals blame themselves; if they believe that bad things happen to bad people; if they believe they have been permanently damaged, and so on. In addition to that, Foa and Kozak (1986) suggest that there is a structure of fear stored in people's long-term memory. This fear structure includes external information and subsequent responses, as well as cognitive appraisals. This means that external information that would otherwise be neutral or even safe connects with negative appraisals and fear responses, therefore creating a sense of uncontrollability.

Finally, Ehlers and Clark (2000) synthesised the above concepts into a model that focuses on:

- the appraisals of the trauma and its consequences (e.g. physical, emotional, occupational, social, etc.);

- the memories of the traumatic event (these are usually visual, and they occur as if they are happening in the here and now);

- the relationship between these memories and the appraisals of the traumatic experience;

- the subsequent behaviours and thinking styles, such as avoidance and rumination;

- the cognitive mechanisms employed during the trauma (e.g., dissociation);

- the details of the trauma, relevant previous belief systems, and the person's general state of well-being.

Cognitive behavioural therapy for PTSD

Following the above, therapy for PTSD follows three main directions: exposure, cognitive restructuring and stress management.

Exposure enables the PTSD sufferers to face their trauma and the situations or people they have been avoiding because of it. The service users expose themselves to the distressing memories in an effort to process them in a more helpful way: that is, to put the memories into perspective, to shape them into more accurate recollections, and to place them in the past. Additionally, people expose themselves to the avoided situations through exposure or in vivo (real-life) exposure.

Cognitive restructuring involves challenging cognitive appraisals and beliefs regarding the trauma, the self, and the avoided situations and people. In therapy, cognitive restructuring techniques and exposure usually interact and are used interchangeably (for an assessment and treatment manual see Foa and Rothbaum, 1998).

Stress management involves skills training. Such skills help deal with high levels of anxiety. Some examples are relaxation techniques and breathing exercises, self-talk (using positive statements, self-reassurance, etc.), assertiveness training, and distraction techniques (for a treatment manual see Meichenbaum, 1997).

Nevertheless, exposure to the traumatic memories and to the places or people that were involved can be very scary and distressing. In its *Guidelines for Good Practice* (BABCP, 2007, p1), The British Association for Behavioural and Cognitive Psychotherapies asserted that:

> *On both ethical and empirical grounds assessments/interventions used will be of demonstrable benefit to the service users both short and long term and will not involve any avoidable loss, deprivation, pain or other source of suffering. It is recognised, however, that circumstances might exist where long term benefits could only be achieved by interventions which involve relatively minor and transient deprivation.*

Consistent with this statement, Wells and Sembi (2004) have developed an alternative treatment plan that bases its rationale on the meta-cognitive model for emotional disorders.

According to these authors, meta-cognition (verbally expressed by meta-cognitive beliefs) manages troubling thinking styles, such as worrying, ruminating, threat monitoring, avoidance and dissociation. The PTSD sufferer employs these mechanisms to cope with the traumatic experience and the subsequent symptoms. However, these mechanisms are counter-productive and increase the symptoms rather than decrease them. Further symptomatology re-activates the meta-cognitive beliefs that trigger further use of the mechanisms. As a result, people become trapped in a distressing loop that they perceive as uncontrollable.

Therefore, meta-cognitive therapy for PTSD targets meta-cognitive beliefs and the cognitive mechanisms involved, rather than the content of the traumatic memories. Alternatively to the exposure techniques, the authors suggest worry postponement, detached mindfulness, attention training and other techniques that help the individual to develop helpful strategies for dealing with the trauma, and for overcoming it (Wells and Sembi, 2004).

C H A P T E R   S U M M A R Y

After exploring the question 'What is anxiety?', this chapter discussed the cognitive, meta-cognitive and behavioural conceptualisations of anxiety and specific anxiety disorders, in addition to assessment, self-monitoring and case formulation issues. Following the introduction of generic anxiety tools such as exposure, a variety of theories and models concerning specific anxiety problems and their relevant therapeutic interventions were discussed. The specific problems covered were phobias, panic disorder, health anxiety, obsessive compulsive disorder and post-traumatic stress disorder. Further reading is recommended for the use of such interventions, as well as appropriate training and clinical supervision to enable their application in clinical practice. Other important features of psychotherapy, such as the therapeutic relationship, have not been discussed in this chapter (see Grant, et al., 2010). Nevertheless this is a crucial element of the therapeutic procedure. Hopefully, this chapter has stimulated you to explore anxiety further, in the spirit of Socrates, who often said that his wisdom was his awareness of his ignorance ('All that I know is that I know nothing').

FURTHER READING

Beck, AT and Emery, G (1985) *Anxiety disorders and phobias: A cognitive perspective.* New York: Basic Books.

This text is not to be missed as further reading for this chapter. Written by the original developer of the cognitive approach, and his early collaborator, this excellent book contains great wisdom for practitioners relatively new to CBT.

Bennett-Levy, J, Butler, G, Fennel, M, Hackmann, A, Mueller, M and Westbrook, D (2004) *Oxford guide to behavioural experiments in cognitive therapy.* Oxford and New York: Oxford University Press.

This was, and is, the first and only book taking a special focus on behavioural experiments for the range of problem areas encountered in general CBT practice. Given that behavioural experiments prove anxiety provoking for mental health practitioners in their early practice of CBT, this book is an essential read.

Butler, G, Fennell, M and Hackmann, A (2008) *Cognitive behavioural therapy for anxiety disorders: Mastering clinical challenges.* New York: Guilford.

This book is a key text to emerge from writer-practitioners of the 'Oxford School'. It would make a good companion text for the Beck and Emery book above.

Craske, MG and Barlow, D (2006) *Mastering your fears and phobias.* Oxford: Oxford University Press.

This is an excellent specialist text focusing, as the cover says, on phobic- and fear-based reactions.

USEFUL WEBSITES

www.padesky.com

This website is a treasure of information about the cognitive behavioural approach, as applied to anxiety-related disorders. It includes many free downloads and very reasonably priced resources, such as training CDs and DVDs.

www.babcp.com

This is the website of the British Association for Behavioural and Cognitive Psychotherapies, the leading organisation for practitioners of the cognitive behavioural approach in Britain. It is a rich source of information, is cheap to join, and includes training events and information about accredited practitioners, trainers and supervisors of the approach.

www.octc.co.uk

This is the website of the Oxford Cognitive Therapy Centre. Training events are advertised here as are many very accessible cognitive behavioural self-help books for clients and mental health practitioners.

Chapter 5

Helping people who are low in mood

Steve Clifford

C H A P T E R   A I M S

After reading this chapter you will be able to:

- appreciate the global impact of depression, as a leading cause of disease, disability and death by suicide;

- understand that classification of depression is not straightforward and may vary according to the perspective taken;

- identify some of the factors that may contribute to the onset, maintenance and prevalence of low mood and depression;

- understand how unhelpful thinking and behavioural patterns can influence mood in a negative manner;

- outline the importance of behavioural activation in alleviating low mood and depression.

Introduction

Everyone experiences times when they feel low in mood and 'depressed'. In our society depression is a word commonly used to describe feeling miserable, fed up or sad. Usually, after a week or two, these feelings lift and we feel happy and contented once again. Sometimes, however, the mood does not appear to lift and can be so extreme that it begins to interfere with everyday life and functioning.

Extreme low mood, or depression, as it is commonly known, is estimated to affect about 121 million people worldwide. The World Health Organisation predicts that by the year 2020 depression will be among the leading contributors to the global burden of disease and it is presently the leading cause of disability worldwide. At its worst, depression can lead to suicide, a tragic fatality, with somewhere in the region of 850,000 lives lost every year (WHO, 2001).

What is depression?

Depression is characterised by severe and persistent low mood. The term 'depression', as typically used in the field of psychiatry, refers to what many CBT practitioners would prefer to call 'extreme low mood' – a more neutral descriptive phrase that does not pathologise people. Depending upon the context, extreme low mood could be normal and adaptive or it could be pathological (Wakefield, et al., 2007). Using the term low mood avoids this distinction.

CHARACTERISTICS OF DEPRESSION

- Low mood *Like a continual deep sadness, 'a big black cloud' engulfs all. Life is joyless and without pleasure. At its worst it is filled with misery and torment.*

- Rumination *The endless repetitive process of going over and over thoughts, ruminating and magnifying things out of all proportion. Thinking too much is like eating too much. The heaviness makes it impossible to remain light and flexible.*

- Hopelessness *Expecting the worst; pessimistic. Often feelings of helplessness and despair can lead people to conclude that nobody can help and they may feel there is no point in talking to anyone about it.*

- Loss of interest *In work and pleasurable activities, coupled with apathy can lead to inactivity.*

- Guilt *Over not being a good enough parent/wife/husband/employee, etc. Feeling guilty over past trivial acts of dishonesty, or the person believing they have committed a heinous crime and deserve to be caught and punished.*

- Alienation *Feeling different from others, not part of society.*

- Loss of confidence *Often accompanied by loss of self-belief and fearfulness.*

- Crying *Easily moved to tears, often with little relief; sometimes depressed people feel beyond tears and unable to cry.*

- Negative outlook *Seeing the black side of things; nothing is positive.*

- Feeling a failure *Successes are discounted or attributed to chance. Depressed people may believe they are failing in everything that they do and that others view them as a failure.*

- Increased anxiety *From worry to fearfulness and often out of proportion to circumstances; frequently accompanied by physical tension and headaches.*

- Emotional numbing *Inability to feel a normal range of emotions and loss of reactivity. Absence of feeling and emptiness.*

- Giving up *Everyday tasks and activities are neglected. People with low mood do less, consequently, the worse they feel the more they give up and the less they do.*

- Irritability and anger *Frustration and shortness of temper can lead to explosive outbursts. This is often completely out of character.*

- Loss of energy and fatigue *Leading to reduced activity.*

- Poor memory *Particularly short-term memory.*

- Loss of concentration *This leads to difficulty focusing on activities such as reading and can affect ability to work. It may also inhibit conversation, promoting hesitancy.*

- Appetite changes *'Comfort eating' or lack of appetite is common.*

- Sleep disturbance *Sleep is frequently broken, often with early morning wakening.*

- Loss of libido *Decline in sexual energy and interest is commonplace.*

- Thoughts of death *Morbid thoughts of death and dying. Death may be viewed as a welcome relief and may progress to thoughts of suicide.*

- Withdrawal *Can magnify over time and the tendency to stay indoors avoiding people is very common. Tasks such as not answering the telephone, opening letters, going shopping or attending social functions promotes isolation.*

The difficulty of classifying depression

One of the difficulties in trying to classify depression is that it can vary from person to person. Some people may experience high levels of anxiety and worry, whilst others might feel persistently low in mood and yet not feel anxious. Some might find that all they want to do is cry or comfort eat. The picture can vary so much. Some features, such as loss of interest and motivation, along with low energy levels, are commonplace. It could be argued that depression is an experience that everyone has from time to time to a greater or lesser degree. Some would suggest that depression is a normal evolutionary adaptive response to events such as loss, with bereavement, redundancy and divorce underpinning many episodes of depression. A recent study published in the *Archives of General Psychiatry* suggests that at least 25 per cent of Americans diagnosed with depression are simply experiencing grief (Wakefield, et al., 2007).

Both depressive feelings and depressive symptoms (Raphael, 1996) have been described in association with bereavement. Keller and Ness (2005) suggest that situational factors play a large role in depression aetiology, also that its severity is proportional to the seriousness of the precipitant. The case study which follows will illustrate this.

CASE STUDY

Most of us will have experienced loss at some point in our lives – for example, Jane had been going out with Jake for six months when he ended the relationship saying that he had another girlfriend. Jane was devastated; she could not stop crying, stopped eating and found it difficult to sleep. Jane found herself consumed with guilt and could not envisage a future without Jake. At times she even thought of killing herself. For two weeks she felt that life had no purpose, but slowly, with the support of friends, her behaviour and symptoms returned to normal.

If we look at the presenting symptoms and apply the DSM-IV-TR criteria, Jane would meet the criteria for a diagnosis of major depressive disorder.

(Keller and Ness, 2005)

The DSM-IV-TR diagnostic criteria

The primary reference for medical diagnosis of depression is the DSM-IV-TR (APA, 2000). It classifies a list of features or 'symptoms':

- depressed mood;
- marked loss of interest or pleasure;
- significant weight change or change in appetite;
- sleep disturbance;
- being agitated or slowed down;

- loss of energy;
- poor concentration and decision making;
- feelings of worthlessness and guilt (not just about being depressed);
- difficulty concentrating and making decisions;
- recurrent thoughts of death or suicide.

If somebody has a single episode of depression this may be classified as a major depressive episode, whereas if they experience frequent bouts of depression, then the condition is referred to as a major depressive disorder. Sometimes people experience a less severe, enduring low mood state – this is often known as dysthymia. In defining this state, the medical establishment traditionally separated depression into two groups: the type of depression that occurred as a result of adverse life events and which could be readily identified – reactive or neurotic; and the other type which appeared to have no readily identifiable cause and seemed to come from within the person – endogenous or psychotic.

Such classification has fortunately now been largely disregarded. Implying that somebody became depressed because they have suffered a major adverse life event, for example, when another person managed to come through a similar life event without becoming depressed, often led to people thinking of themselves as weak in some way. Conversely, to imply that the depression has emerged from within the person and from no exterior source is just as unhelpful, as it may encourage the individual to view themselves as somehow flawed, dysfunctional, or that they must have some weakness of character (Beech, 2003).

Depression can be classified in a number of different ways depending on the frequency and severity of its features (Grant, et al., 2004). There are a number of distinct subtypes, which are in essence clusters of clinical symptoms within differing presentations. The boundaries between subtypes are often fuzzy, with some overlap of symptoms, and not every depression expert agrees on the classification system (Marano, 2002). Examples of subtypes include:

- *Dysthymic disorder*, characterised by an enduring low mood state that occurs for most of the day, more days than not, for at least two years. Individuals describe their mood as sad or 'down in the dumps'. Individuals demonstrate low interest and self-criticism, often seeing themselves as uninteresting and incapable. Because these symptoms have become so much a part of the individual's day-to-day experience, they are often not reported.

- *Bipolar disorder*, previously known as manic depression, is associated with extreme mood swings (mania) giving rise to euphoria and elation, followed by a plummet to extremely low mood (depression). Other symptoms may include grandiose and persecutory delusions, irritability and agitation. These may occur as single or recurrent episodes.

- *Cyclothymic disorder* presents as an enduring, fluctuating mood disturbance involving numerous periods of elevated mood and numerous periods of low mood. Neither, however are of sufficient number, severity or duration to meet the full criteria for a manic episode or for a major depressive episode as classified in the DSM-IV-TR (APA, 2000).

While from a diagnostic perspective there may be clear subtypes or clusters, from a clinical perspective, however, the *meaning* of these symptoms for clients can vary greatly, with no presentation being identical to the next (Grant, et al., 2004). Each person's experience is different and it is vital that this condition we refer to as depression should not simply be reduced to a diagnosis followed by a strict ruled regime of treatment. Classifying depression this way can be very useful for professionals, but trying to group clusters of symptoms into separate boxes does not really portray the individual experience of depression, or indeed adequately embrace the variation and complexity of this condition.

Working together, developing a shared understanding of the clients difficulties, and listening and trying to know just what is going on for them, is the start point. Working 'with them', as they make sense of what is happening and then developing therapeutic interventions together and modifying strategies accordingly, is the way to create a truly therapeutic relationship and one that can really help the depressed person.

CLASSIFICATION – SUMMARY

There is often no clear distinction between low mood and depression. The medical model affords a distinct criterion and classifies extreme low mood as an illness. Whilst convenient, such classification does not capture the variety and complexity of the individual experience.

Different ways of viewing depression

Since the beginning of recorded history, different cultures have ascribed various labels to what we know as depression. In the nineteenth century, it was referred to as Involutional Melancholia, and the term 'depression' did not come into common usage until after the First World War when it first appeared as an 'illness' in Western diagnostic manuals.

What advantages are there in viewing depression as an illness? For some people having a 'label' and knowing they have an 'illness' can be a great relief, rather than just seeing themselves as a failure. Being able to seek treatment from medical professionals and to rely on their expertise enables the handing over of power and responsibility for recovery to somebody else. Nowadays, advances in technology and medical research mean that there are a wide range of pharmaceutical preparations available to address the biological factors contributing to depression, therefore 'popping a pill' offers all the benefits of a 'quick fix' and fits in with our fast-paced society.

The disadvantages of viewing depression as an illness are that individuals become 'passive recipients of care' when they hand over power. In addition, however, handing the responsibility for cure over to the medical establishment means that any responsibility for change in the wider society can be dismissed; as the 'problem' is seen to 'belong' to the 'ill' person, social and other factors need not be addressed. Because depression is a non-contagious condition, such as measles or whooping cough, it is viewed differently to other illnesses and to this day may still be viewed in some quarters as a weakness of character. At the same time, there are many who would not seek help in order to avoid the stigma of an 'illness' label. Viewing depression as an illness tends to place emphasis on medical and psychological aspects; other aspects such as social and environmental factors tend to take a secondary position and this does little to support an inclusive holistic perspective.

Whether or not depression is regarded as an illness, it is important to recognise there are limitations to each perspective. There is much to be gained by keeping an open mind and recognising that, irrespective of position, the relationship between mental health nurse and client is at the heart of the healing process.

Why do people become depressed?

Depression is so prevalent that it can be found across all sectors of society, regardless of sex, gender or age. Throughout the years various theoretical explanations have been put forward to suggest its cause.

Biological perspective

Are we more likely to experience low mood and depression if our parents or grandparent had similar experiences? The answer is probably yes, but the inheritance of mood disorders is complex and we need to look at the whole 'nature versus nurture' argument here. Biologists would assert that our behavioural responses are learnt from our parents as well as our cognitive outlook. For example, if we are taught from an early age that all dogs are dangerous and unpredictable, this will affect the way we relate to dogs (Marks, 1980). If we are conditioned to expect things to go wrong and to view success as a chance event, this too might affect our outlook on life and could predispose us to a negative or anxious mindset. Over time, based on cumulative experiences and predictions about current and future experiences, views become fixed, even when they may be incorrect and biased (Young and Behary, 1998).

Genetic predisposition

Geneticists have identified certain chromosomes – 4, 5, 11, 12, 18 and 21 and the X chromosome – which they consider are causal agents responsible for depression as well as a number of genes, which they say can impact on serotonergic pathways and have been associated with suicide and suicidal behaviour (Du, et al., 2001).

Psychosocial vulnerability

Early life experiences such as sexual or physical abuse or the death of a parent is thought to increase the likelihood of depression in later life (Nemeroff, 2004). Other factors, such as adverse living conditions, loss of job, relationship problems, social isolation and death or illness of a relative, are also thought to make people more likely to become depressed (Bruce, 2002).

Comorbid health conditions

Low mood and depression often accompany other health conditions such as anxiety, rheumatoid arthritis, stroke, cancer and chronic pain. The so-called subtype 'vascular depression' is believed to arise as a result of vascular disease, which may predispose, precipitate or perpetuate depression (Thomas, et al., 2004). It is considered that there is a link between conditions such as cardiovascular disease due to heart rate variability, blood platelet function and hypothalmic-pituitary-adrenal dysregulation (Grippo and Johnson, 2002). Other comorbid health conditions may include thyroid dysfunction, COPD, HIV/Aids, as well as long-term alcohol or substance addiction.

Biochemical theory

Chemical imbalance in the brain is thought to lead to depression, hence the rationale underpinning anti-depressant therapy where specific drugs are given to supposedly correct the imbalance. It is thought that disturbances in the serotonin, noradrenalin and dopamine neurotransmitter systems are responsible, though other mechanisms may also be involved (Nemeroff, 1998; Garlow, et al., 1999).

Psychodynamic theory

This theory suggests that the unconscious and past experiences determine emotional development and current behaviour. For example, a child who was ostracised by peers may have developed the belief that love was dependent on pleasing others. In adulthood, the interpretation that others are displeased might lead to internalised anger, sadness, lowering of mood and subsequent depression. Similarly, someone who endured long periods of illness as a child and was overprotected by their parents may grow up believing they are frail, weak and in need of the support of others. If such support is not forthcoming, they may feel helpless and vulnerable, which in turn may render them prone to depression (Dryden, 2007).

Social explanation

The Social model (Brown and Harris, 1978) suggests that women in particular are susceptible to depression due to social vulnerability. Several contributory areas are thought to increase risk: early maternal loss, young dependent children, absence of confiding relationship and unemployment. While this explanation emphasises external factors, it is the internalisation of emotions associated with these factors that precipitates depression.

Interpersonal dysfunction

Early childhood experiences, growing up in a critical, non-caring environment, a lack of warmth, praise and affection, coupled, perhaps, with being the victim of abuse or bullying at school, can impact significantly on later psychological development. Furthermore, such experiences may lead to the development of a negative self-perception and a negative outlook on life. It can affect the way we relate to others around us and make it difficult to trust and be open. This way of looking at the world has been suggested as a significant factor in the development of low self-esteem (Fennell, 2006) and depression (Barker, 1992).

Behavioural theory

The essence of behavioural theory is that everything amounts to behaviour and that inner processes are of little or no account. So if people feel low in mood and depressed, it is because of their behaviour. Less emphasis is placed on thoughts and emotions and much more upon what can be observed. Behaviourists argue that increasing engagement in behaviours that make someone feel good, whilst reducing those that do not, would have a beneficial effect on the mood (Dryden, 2007; Lewinsohn, et al., 1969).

Cognitive theory

From a cognitive perspective individuals prone to low mood and depression view the world from a negative and self-critical perspective. Beck asserts that it is *not what happens* in the person's

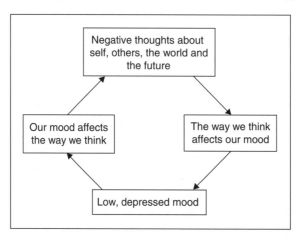

Figure 5.1 The 'vicious cycle' (Marien, 2005)

world that leads to a downturn in mood, but how it is perceived. In other words it is *what they think is happening* that is the crucial factor (Beck, et al., 1979). This type of thinking often follows a downward trend. Such thoughts can create a vicious cycle (see Figure 5.1), where negative thinking leads to negative appraisal and interpretation. This, in turn, leads to negative responses and lowering of mood, followed by further negative thinking, and the cycle continues.

Conclusion

Whilst it can be convenient to point to any one of these theories as the primary causative factor, once we do so we are really narrowing our perspective and adopting a reductionist approach. Rather than accept a simple, unitary explanation, from a CBT perspective it is helpful to look at the different aspects as parts of the whole, and to see how they impact on each other to promote low mood and depression.

CASE STUDY

Jane is in her late teens and is one of three children. Her mother and grandmother both experienced bouts of low mood and depression. Jane's mother is a single parent and has been since Jane's father died. The family live in a part of town where there is high unemployment and social deprivation. Jane herself has been out of work since leaving school. Sometimes Jane has bouts of extreme low mood and finds it hard to commit herself to anything. She attributes this to recurrent back pain from a car accident when she was thirteen, which she says affects her ability to think and concentrate. Some days the pain is so bad she stays in bed all day. Jane feels very pessimistic about the future.

In such circumstances it is clear to see how a complex interplay of factors may contribute to low mood and depression. Indeed, some would say that for many like Jane such low and depressed mood is a reflection of 'misery' and should not be classified as depression at all.

WHY DO PEOPLE BECOME DEPRESSED? – SUMMARY

There is no single cause; often there is an interplay of different factors. A tendency towards low mood and depression often runs in families, while others are more vulnerable because of their environment or the surroundings in which they live. Childhood experiences such as abuse, bullying and loss can be a significant factor as can be major life events. Scientific research points to biochemical changes and physical illness as relevant. The important thing from a CBT perspective is to look at the different aspects as part of the whole, and see how they impact on each other.

Treatment and intervention for depression

For people experiencing low mood and depression there are a variety of different approaches used to help them, but medication and psychological therapies are the most popular methods of managing this condition. The most important start point is to remember that every person will have a different experience and be presenting with different features. Therefore, people should be assessed on an individual basis and interventions should be tailored to address their needs.

Medication

Medication, usually in the form of antidepressants, is most commonly recommended for moderate to severe depression, although studies have shown that antidepressant medication is no more effective than a placebo (or dummy pill) for mild depression (Spigset and Martensson, 1999). In general, medication can be very helpful, particularly if combined with evidence-based psychotherapy such as CBT. There are quite a number of different antidepressants available and these will often be selected for their different qualities, such as whether they are sedating or have stimulant properties, or whether they help reduce anxiety symptoms. Most take about two weeks to start working and sometimes people may need to try several different ones to find which works best. Most have some side effects but these usually will fade within a week or two and are largely bearable. Typical side effects are dry mouth, blurred vision or constipation. Antidepressants are not addictive, unlike many tranquillisers and sedatives (sleeping pills). It has been recommended that people continue to take antidepressant medication for at least four to six months after they are feeling better, in order to minimise relapse (Prien and Kupfer, 1986). When discontinuing medication the dose should be gradually reduced to minimise withdrawal symptoms.

Psychological therapies

There are many forms of counselling and psychotherapy available. Some are better than others for helping people experiencing low mood and depression. Generally speaking, counselling is helpful for specific problems such as relationship difficulties and bereavement where there may be associated low mood. Those with longer-term, recurrent low mood and depression might benefit from a combination of psychotherapy and antidepressant medication. CBT is widely used and is recognised as one of the most effective evidence-based therapeutic approaches for those who suffer from depression.

Research into the effectiveness of CBT spans 40 years and covers uncontrolled clinical trials and nearly 100 randomised controlled trials and effectiveness studies. It concludes that CBT is at least comparable to antidepressant medication and other evidence-based psychological therapies, including interpersonal therapy and behavioural activation. Most outcome research relates to individual CBT, but there is evidence that group CBT is equally effective. Importantly, the beneficial effects of CBT appear to continue up to several years post-treatment and are not only associated with preventing relapse but there is sound evidence that CBT may be superior to continued use of antidepressants in preventing relapse. Trials have also shown CBT to be equivalent to antidepressant medication in the treatment of moderate to severe depression (Kuyken, et al., 2007).

Overall, psychodynamic and psychoanalytical approaches are perhaps less helpful, as they tend to be longer term and encourage people to focus on the past, and for those people who ruminate this may serve to compound rather than alleviate anxiety. These approaches are also financially more costly in view of its longer-term nature.

TREATMENT AND INTERVENTION – SUMMARY

The main interventions used to help people with low mood and depression involve either talking (psychological treatments) or taking medication. The combination of medication and psychological treatment appears to be more effective than one or the other. CBT has been recognised as one of the most effective evidence-based therapeutic approaches for people who suffer with depression.

CBT and depression

CBT is widely recognised as an effective first-line treatment for low mood and depression, and one that works well in conjunction with medication. It is also of value in helping people to avoid relapse, and its effects and benefits carry on even after therapy has ended (Strunk and DeRubeis, 2001). It could be said that CBT provides people with the tools and skills to 'become their own therapist'.

CBT as we know it today embraces both cognitive and behavioural therapies. A common misconception about CBT is that it is primarily a 'talking' therapy and that traditional behaviour therapy is a more practical 'doing' therapy. For example, it might be assumed that a client suffering with low mood and symptoms of anxiety struggling to get out of the house would simply talk to a CB therapist about their concerns and their perception of the difficulties, while a behavioural therapist would actually take them out and encourage them to face their fears. The reality is that the difference between the two is simply one of emphasis. The CB therapist employs tasks and practical-based activities just like the behavioural therapist, but they are employed in such a way as to change thinking. Consider the case of the client struggling to get out of the house, perhaps fearful of being overwhelmed with anxiety and panic. The behavioural therapist 'exposes' her to the feared stimulus on a number of occasions with the aim of 'extinguishing' the fear response. The CB therapist uses a similar practice, but for quite different reasons. Instead of simply exposing the client to the feared stimulus, they would be looking at the client's 'prediction' of what might happen; in other words, what it is that the client fears might happen. In this case, the client fears that they would collapse as a result of overwhelming anxiety and be rushed to hospital. Since the client has stopped going out, this belief is never put to the test and so is understandable.

Together, the worker using the CB approach and the client plan a 'behavioural experiment' to test the prediction. After rating the belief on a 0 to 100 per cent scale, they consider an 'alternative belief' such as I will feel uncomfortable but these feelings will pass, furthermore, I will not collapse and be taken to hospital. Because behavioural change is such a powerful way of changing or modifying beliefs, behavioural tasks (and experiments) are incorporated into CBT and form the cornerstone of this approach. Therefore, the most effective way for someone with low mood and depression to disprove the belief that they cannot do anything is by actually carrying out specific tasks. Completing these tasks directly contradicts the self-defeating belief (Trower, et al., 1995).

While the actual outcomes of CBT will naturally vary from person to person, the main focus for change will be cognition (thoughts) and behaviour. However, emotions and bodily (physiological) sensations are also used as indicators of change, particularly where emotional or physiological disturbance is a major facet of the presenting problem (Dobson and Dozois, 2001). An example of an emotional and physiological presentation would be the case of somebody who has suffered a major loss, is excessively sad and tearful, and has lost significant amounts of weight due to loss of appetite. In this case, therapy focuses on helping people to modify thoughts, which in turn positively influence emotions and bodily state (Sanders and Wills, 2005).

According to Beck, the American psychiatrist who originally developed cognitive therapy back in the 1960s, beliefs formed early in life and shaped throughout our childhood underpin the way we view ourselves, others and our world. Such beliefs develop as a result of our experiences and by adulthood are often firmly held. Together, these three themes are known as the 'cognitive triad'. The themes are prefixed by the words:

> *I am . . . ,*
>
> *Others are . . .,*
>
> *The world is . . .*

Examples of such thinking can be associated with negative perception. For example, if someone is in the grip of depression as a result of job loss, they might hold the beliefs:

I am . . . useless and deserved to be made redundant.

Others are . . . better than me and more deserving.

The world is . . . cruel and unfair.

Often such themes will play out again and again when situations trigger a negative perception of events. Low self-esteem and poor self-worth will often accompany this outlook and the themes associated with such thoughts will be personal to each of us. These beliefs and assumptions form the 'blueprint' or 'frame of reference' for our world view, and will determine the way we relate and interact with others, and how we judge ourselves and the world in general (Beck, 1976; Beck, et al., 2003; Young, et al., 2003).

A related perspective that is very important in shaping our outlook on life is that of the significance of automatic thoughts, assumptions and core beliefs. The cognitive triad could be said to have its origins in our innermost core beliefs (sometimes referred to as schemas). The relationship between thoughts, assumptions and core beliefs is often represented in terms of a metaphor which captures layers of belief (Padesky, 1998), with the outer layer representing automatic thoughts, the middle layer representing underlying assumptions and the centre representing core beliefs (see Figure 5.2).

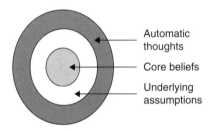

Figure 5.2 (Padesky, 1998)

An alternative, and equally helpful diagrammatic representation, is that of the slippery tree (Figure 5.3), with the leaves representing automatic thoughts, the branches and trunk represent underlying assumptions and the roots representing the core beliefs. Because automatic thoughts can lead rapidly to underlying assumptions, and then activate our core beliefs, the notion of a slippery tree seems an appropriate description.

Every waking moment we have countless numbers of thoughts and invariably they will be accepted as facts and without question. Because thoughts come into our mind without any effort, they are predominantly referred to as 'automatic thoughts'. The lower the mood becomes, the more negative the thoughts tend to be and the more believable they are. From a CB perspective, the aim will be to help clients recognise when they are thinking negatively, to help them look for more realistic or balanced ways of viewing the content of their thoughts, and then to test these out in action.

The next level of thinking relates to what are often called 'underlying assumptions'. The branches and trunk represent the underlying assumptions we make about life. For example, we might grow up with the assumption that the police are there to help us in times of trouble and that they are helpful and supportive. Conversely, we might grow up thinking that the police are only there to stop us if we have done something wrong or to catch us out. Such assumptions will shape our perspective on the world and the way we relate to situations. Along with underlying assumptions there are often rules and standards. An example of a rule might be 'If I am polite then I will be respected.'

Rules or standards such as these often operate without our conscious awareness and we may only be aware of them when other people break or threaten to break them. Provided they are not broken or threatened, we can generally live quite comfortably with them. Rules such as 'If I please people, then they will like me', may stem back to trying to please our parents or significant others. We may move through life trying to please all around us, unaware that we are living by rules developed early in life. It may well be that rules that seemed to work for us as a child have outgrown their usefulness and as adults may actually hold us back. Such rules are activated when, for example, somebody does not obey or follow our rules or does not live up to our standards or expectations. As a result, we may then become unhappy or distressed and could ultimately become depressed. The next level of thinking relates to our core beliefs, which could be viewed as the deep roots of our tree. Often formed early in childhood, these beliefs are powerful and convincing. Our core beliefs are the view we have of ourselves, others and the world.

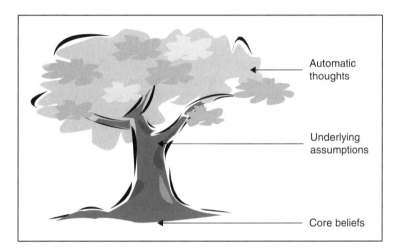

Automatic thoughts

Underlying assumptions

Core beliefs

Figure 5.3 The 'slippery tree' model

Our core beliefs, however, may often be biased and inaccurate, based on a child's eye view of the world (Fennell, 2006). The situations that awaken or trigger our core beliefs are those that are linked to beliefs about ourselves, our rules for living, our standards and the assumptions we make about situations, events and the world. In practice, working with clients helping them to identify the link between thoughts, assumptions and beliefs can really assist them to modify patterns of behaviour and reactions that impact on mood and functioning. Working collaboratively, with clients taking an active role in the therapy process rather than as a passive recipient of care, they can develop strategies for change.

Current thinking in the treatment of depression tends to favour an approach that focuses on behaviour, whilst, at the same time, acknowledging the importance of underlying thinking processes in the establishment and maintenance of low mood and depression. It is known as Behavioural Activation (BA) and is part of the family of Behavioural and Cognitive Psychotherapies. Its emphasis is on engaging in behaviours rather than avoidance, and gaining mastery and pleasure from their completion. It embraces thinking with the emphasis on the *process* of thinking (e.g. ruminating, worry, self-attacking) and helping clients to understand and challenge unhelpful thinking patterns (Veale and Wilson, 2007).

CBT AND DEPRESSION – SUMMARY

This development of CBT has its origins in behavioural treatments developed in the 1950s and 1960s. It proved more effective and gained popularity over psychoanalysis and psychodynamic psychotherapies. Modern CBT embraces a combination of cognitive and behavioural interventions and these are used according to the client's presenting difficulties. CBT is a collaborative approach aiming to teach the client to 'become their own therapist'. Behavioural Activation (BA) is the strategy of choice for people with low mood and depression. Its emphasis is on engaging in behaviours rather than avoidance. It embraces thinking with the emphasis on process and helps clients to challenge unhelpful thinking patterns.

Depression – the downward spiral

As rational beings we cope very well with life's challenges. Our actions are directed by our thoughts and feelings which helps us negotiate any difficulties we may face. For example, if we cut our finger, instinctively we suck it and then look for a plaster. If we have a stomach ache, we usually rub the affected area and perhaps sit quietly with a hot water bottle or take some medicine. Unfortunately, following our instinct this way does not necessarily help to alleviate low mood. Ironically, it can actually make matters worse and magnify the downward spiral into depression. For example, if we feel low in mood and cannot face work, our instinct might be to stay at home and go back to bed. Such action will do nothing to lift our mood and will only make matters worse by leading us to avoid people, situations and activity that could make us feel better. Furthermore, we may have to lie to our boss, and subsequently we may feel guilty and then get behind with our work adding to future stress and tiredness.

Below are some examples of what can magnify the downward spiral if left unchecked:

- *Rumination* The endless repetitive process of going over thoughts, often magnifying them out of proportion.
- *Stinking thinking* The type of thinking that can easily spiral out of control where one thought leads to another, typically feeding into negative thoughts about self and life.
- *Lethargy* Loss of interest and low energy can lead to thoughts such as 'I can't be bothered'. The tendency then is to sit down or stay in bed and do nothing. Hobbies and interests are neglected and everything seems too much.
- *Procrastinating* Putting things off, avoidance, eventually leading to a build up of neglected tasks to the point where they become overwhelming.
- *Withdrawal* The tendency to stay indoors, avoiding people and activities. If unchecked, withdrawal can eventually lead to total isolation.
- *Guilt* Individuals experiencing guilt will find themselves magnifying past trivial acts of wrongdoing or experience unreasonable self-blame.
- *Shame* Often characterised by feelings of unworthiness and incompetence, shamed individuals may feel great humiliation. This can lead to lead to withdrawal and social avoidance.
- *Hopelessness* Expecting the worst, often with thoughts that life is not worth living, may lead to thoughts of suicide.

Thinking patterns that can reinforce low mood and depression

From our earliest childhood we are constantly appraising the world around us. Over time we begin to form opinions and draw conclusions about our world. Our thinking, or more precisely, the way we think, can at times be unhelpful. Whilst we may not be aware of it, if our perception of events is inaccurate, this in turn will impact on the way we interpret events. Moreover, because our behaviour and emotional responses are shaped by our thoughts, such thinking can have a detrimental affect on our mood and view of the world.

From a CBT perspective below are some unhelpful thinking patterns typically experienced by people with low mood and depression.

All or nothing thinking This is where everything is perceived as either right or wrong, black or white, with no middle ground: we either succeed or fail. This is a very rigid way of viewing the world and leaves little room for movement. With this thinking pattern, people are more likely to give up on things if they make a small error than accept that things do not have to be perfect all the time. For example, Sasha had joined a gym and was trying to tone up and get fit. She was doing very well and felt pleased with her progress. It was a friend's birthday and she ate two portions of cake. At once her mood dipped, she told herself she had failed in her healthy-living regime. She subsequently ate another slice and vowed to cancel her gym membership.

Overgeneralisation This is where somebody might draw the conclusion that all cars are unreliable because their car broke down on a couple of occasions, or all dogs are dangerous after having been bitten by a dog. This way of thinking tends to impact on mood when a single negative event is perceived as a never-ending pattern of defeat. Phrases such as 'always', 'never' and 'everybody' are typical of this global way of thinking. For example, Alice was feeling very hurt after her boyfriend went out with another girl behind her back, 'That's it,' she said, 'all men are cheats.'

Mental filter Dwelling on the negative aspects and discounting the positive is often a sign that mental filtering is going on. However plausible it may be, information is disregarded or discounted unless it fits with the person's particular belief. For example, Milly was asked to sing at her school talent show. Afterwards, her form tutor congratulated her on a good performance, particularly, considering it was the first time she had sung in public. For the rest of the evening Milly focused on the phrase 'considering it was the first time you have sung in public' rather than focus on the congratulation.

Mind reading This is when, despite no evidence whatsoever, an assumption is made that others are reacting negatively or have negative motives. For example, Sanjit was giving a lecture to a group of executives when he noticed one of them stifle a yawn. 'That's it', he thought, 'I must be boring.' The reality was that the executive had been awake much of the previous night with his six-week-old baby and was very tired.

Magnification The tendency to blow things completely out of proportion and make mountains out of molehills. For example, Chloe found a dent on the door of her new car, she told herself, 'It is ruined, it will never be the same again, I might as well not bother to look after it anymore.'

Minimisation The reverse of magnification, where individuals minimise or diminish the importance of things. For example, Benji let his friend borrow his new and very expensive acoustic guitar. When it was returned the body of the guitar was warped where it had been left in the sun. 'It doesn't matter,' he said, 'It is only a guitar.' Deep inside he felt bad but refused to acknowledge his hurt.

Labelling Very often people say very unkind things to themselves that they would not say to others, such as if they make a mistake, instead of saying 'I made a mistake' they mutter 'fool' or 'loser'. Such self-talk is often very derogatory and can fuel low self-esteem and erode self-worth. For example, Nina was a newly qualified nurse and frequently had been left in charge of a ward of elderly residents at the nursing home where she worked. The ward was often understaffed and her superiors did not take her concerns about safety seriously. After one resident had a bad fall, she blamed herself; as far as Nina was concerned she was incompetent and had failed in her duty. Some months later she resigned, believing she was not cut out to be a nurse.

Personalising This is where people take ownership for something they were not responsible for, perhaps taking on the blame where others were also involved, saying 'It's all my fault' when others were also at fault and thinking 'It must be me' when clearly it may be down to others. For example, Teresa invited a group of friends round for dinner. Midway through the evening when there was a lull in the conversation, during which she felt uncomfortable and struggled to find something to say. She thought to herself, 'They will think I am a bad hostess if there are silences.' It did not occur to Teresa that it was not all down to her to talk and, had she waited, others would have soon spoken.

Should statements In terms of very critical inflexible thinking, 'shoulds' or 'shouldn'ts', 'musts' and 'oughts', as well as 'have to's' are all examples of the subtle demands people place themselves under as they move through life. Subsequently, when they do not achieve whatever it is they 'should' have done, they very often get cross with themselves and feel great frustration. For example, Mohammed was late for work. He was very apologetic when he arrived and felt angry and resentful. The bus should run on time and the traffic should have been moving faster. After all, someone ought to have predicted the heavy snow shower, surely that was what he paid his taxes for!

REFLECTION POINT

- *Review the different types of thinking patterns described that can reinforce low mood and depression.*

- *Do any of these apply to you in terms of the experiences you have?*

- *The next time you are in a group situation, listen to the conversation around you and see if you can identify unhelpful thinking patterns.*

- *Monitor your own conversation and thoughts. Try to challenge your own unhelpful thinking patterns and adopt a more helpful and realistic perspective.*

THINKING PATTERNS – SUMMARY

Certain unhelpful ways of thinking can be obstructive. Our thinking, or more precisely the way we think can lead to a distorted perspective or view of the world around us. This can result in a negative bias, and subsequently affect us, leading to a lowering of mood.

Working with people experiencing low mood and depression

Initial assessment

The initial assessment provides the mental health worker and the client with an opportunity to meet and begin to explore concerns (Grant, et al., 2004, 2008). This is often a very daunting time for the client and it is crucial that the worker listens in such a way that the client knows they have been listened to and understood. From the outset the worker aims to build a positive relationship, as the quality of the therapeutic relationship is vital to the success of the psychotherapeutic encounter. It is important to really try to understand from the client's perspective what they see as their present difficulties and to establish what is at the heart of the issues they bring. It can be very helpful for both worker and client to begin to draw up a formulation together from the outset. This will help to develop collaborative working and strengthen the therapeutic alliance.

ACTIVITY **5.1**

Consider the following:

- *Why might the therapeutic relationship be vital to the success of the psychotherapeutic encounter?*
- *What are the ingredients of a good therapeutic relationship?*

The case formulation or working hypothesis

The case formulation could be described as a diagrammatic map showing how the various presenting aspects link together. In essence, it is a working hypothesis which can give an overview of the presenting difficulty and the connection between the different aspects. It is a way of presenting a picture as a means of understanding, predicting and normalising what people experience (Grant, et al., 2008; Sanders and Wills, 2005). It may begin as an outline with just a few details and can be updated and modified throughout the course of therapy as new aspects emerge. There are many different ways in which a formulation for low mood can be constructed, and one example of a simple formulation is a series of lines and arrows that show the way thoughts and feelings are linked together. In Figure 5.4, we can see how, as a result of him waking up feeling low in mood and physically tired, John thinks to himself 'I'm going to have another bad day.' He makes a prediction. As a result, he decides to stay in bed and, consequently, he feels even more fed up having achieved nothing and wasted a day in bed.

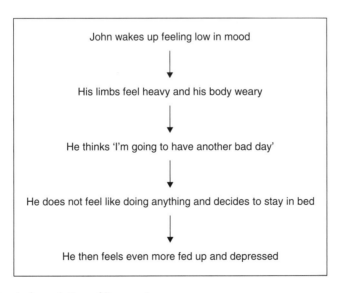

Figure 5.4 A simple formulation of lines and arrows

Another way of formulating the same information is using a three column A, B, C format (Figure 5.5).

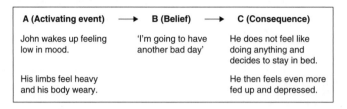

Figure 5.5 Same information in a three column format

As you will begin to notice, we are mapping out the different aspects and separating events, beliefs and consequences. Figure 5.6 provides another way of showing the same information.

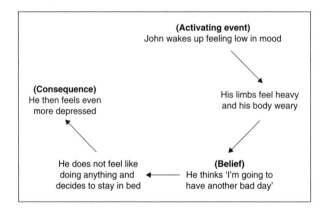

Figure 5.6 Another formulation of the information

If you look at the formulations again, you will see how we could change the labels from events, beliefs and consequences to thoughts, emotions (feelings), physical aspects and behaviour. Figure 5.7 provides the same formulation as Figure 5.6 but with labels changed.

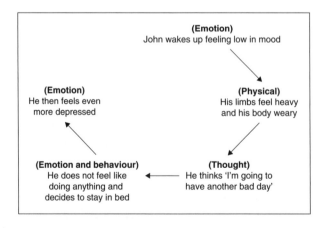

Figure 5.7 Formulation with change to labels

Figure 5.8 shows another way of drawing a formulation that illustrates the way all thoughts, emotions (feelings), physical aspects and behaviour link together. This method is known as the 'three systems approach' (Rachman and Hodgson, 1974, from Grant, et al., 2004).

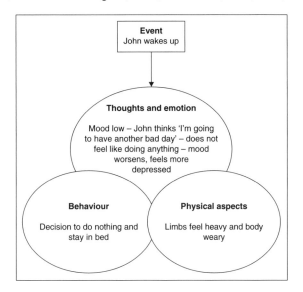

Figure 5.8 The three systems approach

Finally, to illustrate the many different ways information can be presented, Figure 5.9 presents a model that incorporates the individual's environment. The term 'environment', in John's case, is waking up at home, alone.

You will note that the other four parts of the model in Figure 5.9 – *thoughts, emotions, physical* and *behaviour* – are contained within the circle representing the *environment*. This is to show how these four parts make better contextual sense within the overall context of the environment. In other words, the environment sets the scene in which the action happens.

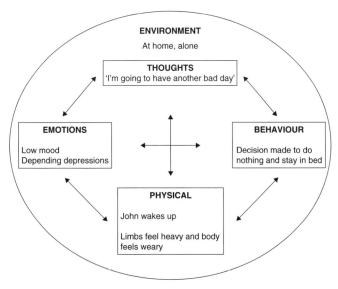

Figure 5.9 The five-part model (Padesky and Mooney, 1990)

The five-part model is a very popular and helpful formulation for use with people who are experiencing low mood and depression. It has also been given the nickname 'hot cross bun' and you will note that the lines separating the different aspects also connect them. This shows how each is connected to the other. According to Padesky and Mooney (1990), just as changes in any one of these parts can make you feel worse, equally such changes can make you feel better. In John's case, the area to change is *behaviour* and, from a cognitive behavioural perspective, if John decided to get up instead of staying in bed, his mood would lift and his physical state would improve. Furthermore, he would most likely discover that his feared 'bad day' was in his imagination.

FORMULATION – SUMMARY

A formulation is a developing hypothesis or blueprint. It is 'work in progress' and ideally will develop throughout the course of therapy as client and therapist uncover and gain a greater understanding of the presenting difficulties. A formulation may also highlight strengths and can be subject to change according to circumstances. 'Off the peg' formulations can be used, as can simple home-made diagrams.

Measures

In order to monitor progress, various measures may be used – these can be standardised such as the *Beck Depression Inventory* (BDI 11) (Beck, 1996), or *General Health Questionnaire* (GHQ) (Goldberg and Hillier, 1978). These represent tried and tested, reliable measures and can be broad or specific in focus. Person-specific measures can also be used and can be as simple as asking, 'On a scale of 0 to 100, with 0 representing extremely depressed, can you rate your mood?' Such measures can be taken every session or at intervals throughout therapy. At the first session, measures are usually introduced to obtain a 'baseline' from which to monitor progress (Grant, et al., 2004, 2008).

Behavioural activation

Symptoms related to low mood, such as loss of interest, motivation and pleasure often coincide with tiredness and lethargy to produce a state of inactivity. In extreme cases, people may take to their beds and avoid most or all activities in an attempt to obtain relief from symptoms. Paradoxically, reduction in activity serves to reinforce and maintain low mood, particularly when coupled with negative ruminations. Avoiding opportunities to engage in meaningful activities and contact with others invariably leads to people feeling alone, and can fuel low self-esteem and reinforce lack of worth and poor self-image.

An inevitable consequence of inactivity and lack of motivation is neglect, not only in terms of self-care and personal hygiene, but also avoiding responsibilities at work or home. This may begin by putting off tasks such as opening letters and answering correspondence. Important engagements may be missed and people avoided. Ultimately, this may lead to bills going unpaid, employment difficulties and withdrawal from almost all activities. Everyday activities such as tidying, cooking and shopping may become too much as everything begins to pile up until it all feels totally overwhelming. Unfortunately, the guilt and perception of failure brought about as a result of neglect and withdrawal can lead to a further lowering of mood, and in some cases this may even lead to thoughts of suicide.

From a CBT perspective we can see how a vicious cycle develops: low mood leads to negative

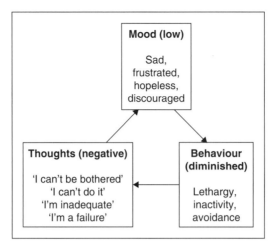

Figure 5.10 The 'vicious cycle' that maintains low mood and depression

thoughts, which in turn leads to inactivity (Figure 5.10). The mood lowers further and discouragement fuels the cycle.

Studies have shown that behavioural activation can be very effective in helping people who are experiencing low mood relating to depression (Jacobson, et al., 1996), including those with more severe depression (Dimidjian, et al., 2006). By increasing activity levels, doing more and including pleasurable activities, people begin to feel better and, over time, this will have a direct impact on the mood, improving well-being and reversing the downward spiral.

The value of increased activity

When a person is experiencing low mood, they are likely to feel low in energy, they may spend much of the time sitting or laying around, perhaps doing very little. This is not helpful and contributes to lethargy and tiredness. Furthermore, if they are not engaged in meaningful activities, it is likely that they will be ruminating on negative thoughts – a sure-fire way to deepen an already low mood. Increasing activity levels helps people to feel more energised and less tired. It can help to promote a better quality of sleep and stimulate appetite.

Increased confidence

Being active helps to rebuild confidence and self-esteem. Setting oneself a task and achieving it can lead to a sense of accomplishment. As the successes grow with more tasks completed, the mood will most certainly lift as people feel that they are beginning to take control of their life once again. They will be more inclined to try things if they are seeing results and the knock-on effect is that motivation levels will also rise. This will also generate a sense of hope in those around them.

Keep it simple

It is far better to succeed in a small way than to fail monumentally. Somebody with extreme low mood may well find even the smallest of tasks overwhelming. The key to successful behavioural activation is to keep it simple. Setting a goal such as getting out of bed and sitting in an armchair is far better than expecting clients to get out of bed, wash, dress, shave and then sit in the armchair. Starting off with a small task and then adding another over time is the way to achieve success. Another factor to consider is the impact of negative thinking, as often the depressed person may harbour thoughts such as 'I won't be able to do this', or 'I know I will fail.' Thoughts such as these make it really difficult to start doing anything, and so small achievable steps are vital.

Increase positive feelings

Doing things that will increase fun and pleasure will help to increase positive feelings. It is important to get a balance and to include a mixture of chores and pleasurable activities. Where tasks can be set that achieve more than one outcome, these are especially worthwhile – for example, those that afford a sense of mastery and achievement as well as pleasure. Tasks may include something as simple as preparing and putting a bunch of flowers in a vase, where the end result is something that has been accomplished and also looks nice, or having a leisurely bath or going out to meet a friend for coffee. All these activities are pleasure-based rather than simply chores or tasks.

Increase activity levels in graduated steps

Just like the training involved in preparing to become a marathon runner or mountaineer, the aim should be to slowly increase the number of activities, breaking tasks down into small achievable steps and gradually building up. Tidying up one shelf of a cupboard, rather than the whole cupboard or tidying one work surface rather than the whole kitchen in one go, is the way to ensure successful completion of goals. Sometimes engaging in an activity for a set period of time is a workable alternative to completing tasks in their entirety – for example, reading a newspaper for five minutes rather than reading the entire newspaper.

Include physical exercise

Where possible, include a mix of physical-based activities. Examples might include a short cycle ride, a walk round the park, vacuuming the carpet or mowing the grass. Hippocrates, the Greek philosopher and founder of medicine, in 400 BC recommended exercise, describing walking as 'man's best friend'. Physical activities will help to improve all-round health, promote sleep, stimulate appetite and increase energy levels. It will allow the body to work off tension and stiffness, as well as releasing frustration and anger. Also, physical activity helps increase the blood flow to the brain, which serves to stimulate the release of naturally occurring mood enhancing hormones known as endorphins.

Using a programme or timetable

It can be really helpful to write down a daily programme or timetable. Having a visual record will assist you in monitoring and reviewing progress with your client. It can also help with planning and structuring activities. It can also help if the client is able to rate their mood on a simple 0 to 10 scale each day, perhaps marking this on the programme or timetable. Here is an example of a daily timetable for a client who has become very withdrawn and has both low energy levels and poor motivation. He gets anxious socialising and going out of his house.

Daily timetable

Name: *John Smith*

Day/Date: *Monday 3 February*

Time	Planned activity	Comments	Mood rating 0–10		
			Before	During	After
9.00 a.m.	*Get out of bed tired*	*Difficult*	*2*	*2*	*2*
9.05 a.m.	*Wash/shave*	*Successful*	*2*	*2*	*3*
9.20 a.m.	*Get dressed*	*Successful*	*3*	*3*	*4*
9.30 a.m.	*Breakfast*	*No appetite*	*3*	*3*	*4*
9.45 a.m.	*Make bed*	*Hard work*	*3*	*4*	*5*
10.00 a.m.	*Shop/paper*	*Anxious*	*3*	*4*	*6*
10.30 a.m.	*Phone mum*	*Relieved after*	*4*	*5*	*6*
11.00 a.m.	*Sudoku*	*Done it!*	*5*	*6*	*7*
12.00 p.m.	*Lunch*	*Little appetite*	*6*	*6*	*6*
12.30 p.m.	*Rest*	*Enjoyed*	*6*	*6*	*6*
1.30 p.m.	*Tidy cupboard*	*Pleased after*	*6*	*7*	*8*
2.00 p.m.	*Rest*	*Satisfying*	*8*	*8*	*7*
3.00 p.m.	*Tea/snack*	*Enjoyed*	*8*	*8*	*8*
3.30 p.m.	*Listen radio*	*Concentration low*	*7*	*6*	*7*
4.30 p.m.	*Prepare meal*	*Negative thoughts*	*7*	*5*	*6*
5.00 p.m.	*Eat meal*	*Enjoyed*	*6*	*7*	*8*
5.30 p.m.	*Tidy kitchen*	*Pleased after*	*8*	*8*	*8*
6.00 p.m.	*Television*	*Feel tired*	*7*	*7*	*7*
9.00 p.m.	*Pyjamas*	*Feel tired*	*7*	*7*	*7*
9.30 p.m.	*Read book*	*Concentration low*	*7*	*7*	*7*
09.45 p.m.	*Reflection*	*Some success*	*7*	*8*	*8*
10.00 p.m.	*Bed*	*Sanctuary!*			

Figure 5.11 Example of a daily timetable

ACTIVITY **5.2**

Working with a partner, make a list of activities that you might include in a behavioural activation programme. They should ideally be a mix of pleasurable, physical and task-related mastery activities.

Anticipate setbacks

It is important to be flexible and to accept that setbacks will occur, particularly on days when the mood is lower or if a lot of activity has occurred on the previous day. This is one of the reasons why small graduated steps are so important to prevent 'boom and bust'. On such occasions the key is to adjust the level of activity accordingly and to simply note the emerging pattern.

All steps are positive steps

No matter how small, the fact that activity is happening means that positive action towards activating a change of mood is happening. Remember, when the mood is low, motivation does not come about by simply sitting in the armchair, it comes about when doing things.

C H A P T E R S U M M A R Y

Extreme low mood or depression is widespread; it has a profound impact on health and is a leading cause of disability worldwide. Depression is so prevalent that it can be found across all sectors of society, regardless of sex, gender or age. It is characterised by features such as low mood, negative outlook, hopelessness and a lack of energy and motivation. The distinction between low mood and depression is not always clear. There are different ways of viewing depression and limitations to each perspective. Various theoretical explanations have been put forward to explain its cause, including early life experiences, chemical imbalance, genetic predisposition, physical illness and thinking patterns.

Rather than accept a simple, unitary explanation, it is helpful from a CBT perspective to look at the different aspects as parts of the whole, and to see how they impact on each other to promote low mood and depression. CBT addresses unhelpful thinking patterns (cognitions) and behaviour. The intervention of choice is known as Behavioural Activation (BA). The emphasis of BA is on engaging in behaviours rather than avoidance, and gaining mastery and pleasure from their completion. Research studies have shown that CBT used together with antidepressants is more effective than either treatment alone, and that CBT leads to a reduction in future relapse. The quality of the therapeutic relationship is vital to the success of the psychotherapeutic encounter. Careful assessment, using formulation to guide therapy and measures to monitor progress, coupled with collaborative working, ensures that therapist and client are both fully involved in the therapeutic process.

FURTHER READING

Gilbert, P (1997) *Overcoming depression. A self-help guide using cognitive behavioural techniques.* London: BCA.

Gilbert's book is an excellent step-by-step guide for depressive sufferers, to help them both understand and cope more effectively with their disorders and to understand their contextual bases. As well as covering the comprehensive range of CB knowledge and skills, Gilbert provides an evolutionary perspective in terms of social approval, ranking and subordination.

Grant, A, Mills, J, Mulhem, R and Short, N (2004) *Cognitive behavioural therapy in mental health care.* London: Sage Publications Ltd.

Grant, A, Townend M, Mulhern, R and Short, N (2010) *Cognitive behavioural therapy in mental health care.* 2nd edition. London: Sage Publications Ltd.

In this book, and in the 2004 edition, Grant and colleagues provide an excellent overview of CBT for depression and several case studies which well illustrate cognitive and behavioural interventions for the disorder.

Hammen, C (1997) *Depression.* Hove: Psychology Press Ltd.

This text is broad-ranging and covers: definition; diagnosis; depression course and consequence; the biological bases of depression; cognitive and life stress approaches to depression; the social aspects of depression, and biological and psychological treatments.

USEFUL WEBSITES

www.padesky.com

This website is a treasure of information about the cognitive behavioural approach, as applied to depression-related and other disorders. It includes many free downloads and very reasonably priced resources, such as training CDs and DVDs.

Chapter 6

Helping people who hear voices and have false beliefs

James Sullivan

C H A P T E R   A I M S

After reading this chapter you will be able to:

- understand that CBT for distressing and false beliefs can be a valuable tool to improve quality of life, raise self-esteem and reduce the possibility of relapse;

- appreciate more the unique challenges experienced while working with this client group;

- understand the importance of time spent working the client–therapist bond instead of the client's problems directly;

- (in relation to the last bullet point) appreciate the importance of the process of therapy when working with this client group.

Introduction

Cognitive therapy for the resolution of some of the experiences termed 'psychotic' is a comparatively recent innovation, lagging long behind both mood and anxiety disorders in its development. As the greatest proportion of symptoms relevant to this area – false beliefs and hallucinations – will likely be experienced by individuals diagnosed with 'schizophrenia', this chapter will begin with a brief discussion of some of the charges laid against the usefulness of this diagnosis.

Criticism of the concept of schizophrenia

The attitude to schizophrenia among both lay people and professionals has long been qualitatively different from that of other forms of mental disorder and the nature of the diagnosis has been critically examined from many different quarters. The perspective of many voices (Bentall, 1990; Boyle, 1990) currently is that the concept of schizophrenia is suspect and overdue a review. However, this is by no means a 'new' perspective, forming as it did a significant part of the anti-psychiatry movement of the 1960s (e.g. Szasz, 1960).

Current critiques of the schizophrenia construct rest on the argument that all disorders within the medical model are agreed to be a common phenomenon by consensus of presentation in three areas: aetiology, symptomatology and prognosis. The first of these, aetiology, is the study of causal factors in illness and here is where the construct of schizophrenia reaches its first obstacle.

As a disorder, schizophrenia has no definite causative factors. In itself, this fact is not sufficient to dispute the case for building these symptoms into a cohesive mental disorder, after all the cause of all illnesses were once unknown and many still are without facing the same level of scrutiny of their validity. Second, the symptoms or set of symptoms that are unique to the 'schizophrenia' illness is questioned as being inconsistent at best. The diagnostic criteria of each disorder, mental or physical, are outlined in regularly updated disease classification systems, such as the *Diagnostic and Statistical Manual* (APA, 2000) or the International Classification of Diseases (ICD) published by the World Health Organisation (WHO, 1992). The ICD entry for schizophrenia continues to be based upon the hugely influential work of Schneider (1959) who described what have come to be known as the 'first rank' symptoms of schizophrenia.

Schneider's first rank symptoms

- Hearing thoughts spoken aloud

- Third-person hallucinations

- Hallucinations in the form of commentary

- Somatic hallucinations

- Delusional perceptions

- Thought insertion

- Thought broadcasting

- Thought withdrawal.

These symptoms appear in clinical presentation far less often in textbook fashion than one would hope; indeed, numerous instances of cases deviating from the clinical norm have been described in the academic press. As noted above, the set of symptoms that form any illness need to be unique to that illness in their form or when combined; it has been widely noted that this is not the case with the first-rank symptoms above which may appear in differing (predominantly) psychotic illnesses.

Finally, prognosis goes no further towards establishing a clear diagnostic picture, with no clear way to establish the clinical outlook for the individual beyond evidence of some behaviours and experiences that may heighten the potential for relapse. These include substance misuse (Swofford, et al., 1996), major life stress (Nuechterlein, et al., 2007), further subsequent mental health problems (Eaton, et al., 1998), among many others. It may be said that the concept of an illness, within the medical model, is the sum of our current knowledge of the relevant aetiology, symptomatology and prognosis. A deficit in our knowledge of any one area is not enough to bring into question the construction of the disorder but significant question marks over each of these three parts has done so for schizophrenia. That said, the concept of schizophrenia is a hardy one and is unlikely to be modified in the near future by any of the major stakeholders in mental health despite the above outlined criticisms, and the increasingly compelling evidence that simple changes to terminology can reduce stigma (Kingdon, et al., 2008). Beyond these issues, as a broad referent term for professionals indicative of a spectrum of possible symptoms when appended to the individual, 'schizophrenia' could still be argued to be of some limited use. However, in the longer term and barring any significant refinement of the symptomatology of what it actually means to be 'schizophrenic', it seems destined to go the way of terms such as 'insanity' and the 'nervous breakdown'.

Consequently, whilst acknowledging the charges levelled against this concept in each of the three areas of disease classification and the stigmatising attitudes of many within the lay community to 'schizophrenia', it would be beyond this book's remit to further explore these contentious issues. Therefore we shall turn to what CBT can do to resolve distress related to the experiences that form psychoses.

CBT for worrying beliefs

It should first be emphasised that CBT is not a 'cure' for the problems defined as schizophrenia or for any of the psychotic disorders. What it can do, to a limited extent dependent upon the solidity of the therapeutic relationship and the influence this bears upon successful engagement and collaboration, is reduce the distress caused by unusual experiences. Steel (2008) suggests that psychosis is associated with (unusual) 'experiences being interpreted as negative, threatening and external'. In essence CBT seeks to place these experiences within the spectrum of 'normal' human experience.

ACTIVITY **6.1**

Many people's lives are defined by experiences that cannot be quantified or in any sense proven to be 'truth'. There are many examples of this, perhaps you can think of some? Include some from your own life.

A cognitive perspective of worrying belief formation, refinement and perpetuation may be found in Mills, et al. (2004a). This model relies on the impact of *inference*, which we return to frequently. Figure 6.1 shows the process Mills proposes.

The cyclic pattern in Figure 6.1 results in a potential for a spiralling down into further anxiety-provoking thought patterns and other psychotic experiences as it increases stress (see Figure 6.2 stress/diathesis model).

Traditionally, delusions have been defined as false, fixed beliefs. This was certainly the case when the author of this chapter was a student psychiatric nurse, but it may be argued that the reality of

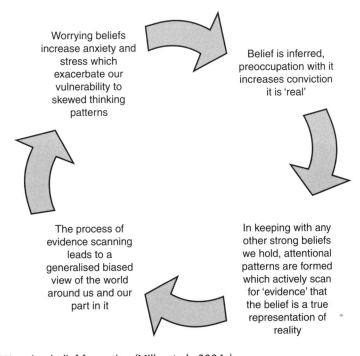

Figure 6.1 Worrying belief formation (Mills, et al., 2004a)

the clinical presentation of delusions is often neither fixed nor necessarily false. It has often been noted that delusions do change spontaneously over time without the influence of either psychotherapy or medication. Also, delusions need not be false. Imagine that an acute ward in-patient observes a nurse walking past his room and thinks, 'She thinks she's better than me, she's trying to keep me down.' This may be a true observation yet remains delusionary when based on the evidence before the client at that time. The Diagnostic and Statistical Manual (DSM) of the American Psychiatric Association states that 'when a false belief involves a value judgement (as this example does) it is regarded as a delusion only when generalised biased patterns are formed . . . so extreme as to defy credibility' (APA, 2000). While the nurse in question may indeed think she is better than the client in question, the evidence for this and the subsequent evaluation that she is actively trying to keep the individual 'down' is not, in the absence of supporting information, credible.

However, the concept of establishing 'truth' in CBT may be, more often than not, unhelpful because it depends on the individual client and clinician's judgements, which are in turn built upon a bedrock of individual experience and beliefs. Clearly we are unlikely to share a universal common perception of a particular event or experience and form exactly the same beliefs with anyone, even close family members, so the chances of this happening with a relative stranger whom we only meet for CBT are vanishingly small. Side-stepping the idea of truth and focusing instead on the usefulness of the belief to the individual allow the potential for frank and open discussion beyond the usual entrenched positions. Often this is a revelation to clients who have been told for many years that their beliefs are wrong, or who have found these topics have simply not been open for discussion with mental health staff who have been trained in the idea that discussing these beliefs with clients is unhelpful or only serves to further entrench a sense of certainty in the delusional idea. As we shall see, this is not the case.

From a cognitive perspective, the driving force behind delusions and the true kernel of the problems they cause individuals is not the inferential belief itself but the consequences this triggers. We may believe anything of anything that we can imagine but if doing so does not interfere in our lives or leave us feeling compelled to act on this 'knowledge', then there must be little problem attached to so believing. Mostly we experience inferences as automatic thoughts which may be difficult to 'catch' for the individual in the moment, although this is a skill like any other that may be taught and mastered.

We can illustrate the importance of inference by returning to our previous example: as our nurse walks past the patient's room, the client takes the evidence presented to him (person walking past his room) and forms the hypothesis (inference), 'She thinks she's better than me.' As noted above, this inference may or may not be true, yet remains unchallenged. Whether accurate or not, the consequences for the individual will almost certainly be distressing, based as they are on specific meaning attributions (see box below). Feelings of shame, embarrassment or anger, among others, may be experienced and behavioural outcomes may vary from avoidance to confrontation.

FORMS OF ATTRIBUTION

- External attribution *The system which places nurses 'above' me is unreasonable.*
- Internal attribution *I'm not as good as her.*
- Unstable attribution *She just thinks she's better than me at the moment.*
- Stable attribution *She'll always think that way about me.*
- Specific attribution *It's just that nurse who sees me this way.*
- Global attribution *Everyone sees me this way.*

(Adapted from Beck, 1976)

Part of the reason for this variance in outcomes from the same delusionary belief in different people may lie in the process of attribution. Another possible reason for a variety of responses to the same cognition in different individuals is the unique rules, conditional beliefs or underlying assumptions relevant to the situation. Rules regarding expectations of others showing respect, for example, will necessitate an appraisal of whether the nurse's behaviour in passing by is respectful. Expectations of what the unwitting nurse *should* have done in order to maintain the patient's rule will vary widely dependent as they are on many variables. Obviously underlying the rule level are core beliefs which may be inferred by a closer examination of the themes inherent in the distressing beliefs, which will be discussed in greater detail later. Suffice it to say for now that many people find their first exposure to the levels of cognitive processes confusing.

Stress and vulnerability

A normalising perspective of false beliefs will focus on these phenomena as existing on a continuum with all other human experiences modified only by one's potential predisposition and current and historical exposure to stress. There are many stressors that will increase the likelihood of anyone having the kind of experiences that society terms 'psychotic'. The difficulty lies in those times when the appraisal of these experiences results in unhelpful consequences. The influence of vulnerability is less well understood but is equally important and the difficulty in predicting an individual's vulnerability to psychosis, at least in part, in the previously mentioned problem (see introduction) of establishing a useful theory of aetiology. Suffice to say that each one of us has a degree of vulnerability to experiencing these types of problems and there are some circumstances that would result in most people having first-hand knowledge of such difficulties. Examples of these situations would include torture, prolonged sleep deprivation, interrogation and even bereavement.

One of the first texts to place 'psychotic' perceptual abnormalities against the background of all other human experiences was that of Zubin and Spring (1977) who produced the rough model outlined in Figure 6.2. This shows the potential for all of us to pass the threshold indicated and experience potentially problematic perceptions. This model should be thought of as a sketch of the territory of unusual human experiences and not a definitive 'road map'. But discussions around this model will often do much to shift the perspective of the conversation away from conceptions of incurable illness and on to one of practical measures to ameliorate the problematic experiences impact. For example, if an individual has had previous psychotic experiences, this will increase vulnerability to further similar experiences. Equally people who appraise their life as greatly stressful will be at greater risk.

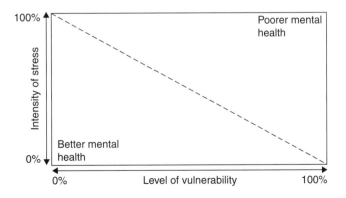

Figure 6.2 Stress diathesis model (Zubin and Spring, 1977)

REFLECTION POINT

When outlining the stress vulnerability model with a client, as with any other theory, it is important to be aware of your own feelings towards it in order to put it across comprehensively and
clearly. Take some time to consider to what extent this theory matches your own beliefs about
the causes of psychotic experiences.

Where would you currently fit within it? How far have you moved up and down it in the past?
What other factors can you think of that could increase stress and exacerbate vulnerability? What
do you think your responses would be to the factors you have identified? How far do you think
they would alter your positioning within the model?

Both of these factors work together to bring about mental health problems. However, it is theo-
retically possible to have a very high vulnerability but minimal stress levels (or vice versa) and
remain well, though, were this the case, any comparatively minor change or life event might
change the clinical picture considerably.

Interventions focus on reducing current stressors, reducing vulnerability or inoculating the individual against adverse or excessive responses to future stresses. To illustrate these differing strands of
input let's consider a client with paranoid ideation leading to an avoidance of social situations.
Ranking high among the list of current stressors might be social isolation. Sensitively and coopera-
tively seeking to increase the list of positive social contacts may reduce stress, but could as a
stand-alone technique be counter-productive as it does nothing directly to target the client's
thoughts of being at risk in social situations. However, a re-appraisal of the utility of holding such
thoughts and their underlying rules and core beliefs will serve to reduce the client's vulnerability
while encouraging the individual to engage in behavioural experiments of this kind.

In tandem with interventions such as this, it is essential to seek out longer standing protective factors appropriate to the individual's circumstances and interests – for example, introducing the
client to a local mindfulness group could establish positive social contacts which may decrease the
possibility of a future return to isolation whilst reducing current stress levels. Taking a collaborative and eclectic approach to experiments may generate solutions beyond the usual provision of
mental health services, which may better engage the client's interests while also integrating the
individual to the community they feel detached from.

Early intervention

Recent research (Morrison, et al., 2004) has indicated that the length of the prodrome (or initial,
untreated duration of schizophrenia) is significant to the clinical outcome of the illness, affecting
both the intensity of the initial episode and the likelihood of subsequent relapses. Consequently,
early detection and intervention is essential to minimise the potential of chronic illness developing. CBT has been shown to be an effective intervention in these vital early stages (Gumley, et al.
2003; Jackson, et al., 2005) and in preventing relapse into subsequent psychotic episodes
(Birchwood, et al., 2000).

Engagement and collaboration

In practice, the primary difficulty with CBT for worrying beliefs is the most basic problem with all
therapy – gaining a commitment from the client to turn up for appointments and take part in the
process. As mentioned earlier, clients may see therapy as revelatory, but equally may treat it with
suspicion or as another method for others to impose their will or beliefs upon them. There may be
many reasons why this is the case, among which may be the previously mentioned perspective

that delusions are not up for discussion with mental health professionals. Alternatively, the nature of the individual's disorder may adversely affect the potential for engagement. Often delusions may be accompanied by a sense of paranoia as we will discuss later. In addition to this possibility, the so-called negative symptoms of schizophrenia may have a de-motivating effect. Socially, beyond these issues, clients may have been told by family members or significant others that they are chronically sick, that medication is the only thing that can help them and so on.

In essence, the most important tool in the therapist's armament in working with these problems is an open flexible attitude and a willingness to discuss the client's perspective without prejudice. The clinical reality of this may be therapy sessions that deviate significantly from that which may typically be expected from a CBT session. The primary focus must always be, as with any such psychotherapy, the wishes of the client. Collaboration is impossible without engagement after all and engagement will only be achieved if the client trusts that their concerns and beliefs are being treated as worthy of investigation without preconceptions.

It is important to be aware that the process of engagement and collaboration is often a lengthy and ongoing undertaking with this client group, taking up to many months, and may be undermined in a matter of moments by a misplaced or inarticulate remark. Consequently, it is vital to remain aware of the early signs of therapeutic breakdown or misunderstanding as these may be the only indications the therapist gets prior to disengagement. Even in more generalised (and less cognitively challenging) mental health services, the drop-out rate among patients with psychosis is estimated at 25 per cent (Kendrick, et al., 2000). Interestingly, despite the more challenging nature of CBT, drop-out rates are often significantly less than in more generalised primary or secondary care services (Kuipers, et al., 1997; Morrison, et al., 2004).

Skills such as feedback, actively checked for accuracy with the client throughout the time spent together, are vital. It is also every bit as essential to seek feedback as to provide it, including a receptive non-defensive attitude to clients' criticisms. More specific questions such as 'What did you find most useful about today's session?', 'In what way do you believe this therapy can help you?' and 'How did you feel about coming to today's session?' may elicit unexpected results at times but will always prove helpful guides for how to tailor the next therapy session in collaboration with the client.

As a footnote to this, it seems to be often the case (Lecomte, et al., 1999) that by the time a client with a diagnosis of schizophrenia is considered receptive to CBT by the referring party, they may often have significant difficulties with social situations and inferring what is and is not 'illness' in their thinking patterns. Low self-esteem is a well-recognised outcome of a diagnosis of schizophrenia (Haddock and Slade, 1996) and CBT has demonstrated efficacy with resolving this problem in this client group (Hall and Tarrier, 2003). Additionally, low self-esteem may have a role in maintaining the presence of worrying beliefs and hallucinations (Garety, et al., 2001). Social anxiety is not generally allied to a sense of paranoia and this state of affairs may or may not be the case in this diagnostic group, consequently – as in working with people with other types of problems – it is important to establish and accurately formulate underlying causes for problems experienced. Where appropriate, often a simple process of normalising experiences (see below), perceived by the client as possibly indicative of their problem skewing their thinking, will assist in both outlining the area of intervention covered by CBT and reinforcing the early stages of engagement. Beyond this, a firm sense of how the lived experience of residual or active symptoms of psychosis, both negative and positive, affect each area of everyday life for the individual is clearly essential in order to tailor therapy to individual circumstances and client-identified goals.

Assessing the problem

The early therapy sessions with people experiencing distressing beliefs are generally significantly less formal in their structure than may be the case with people presenting with differing problems. The reasons for this we have in part discussed above; typically the client may have experienced many years of being told they are a 'schizophrenic', are ill, need help (help almost exclusively meaning medication in such instances) and so on. In light of this, it is perhaps unsurprising that the client may be experiencing a wide raft of emotions on attending their first meeting with you. An open and honest exploration of these feelings is generally the first stop, in tandem with discussion of previous mental health contacts the client has found both helpful and unhelpful.

This may serve to build trust and assess the emotions of the individual new to CBT. However, the clearly definable meanings of emotional states may be difficult for the client and mental health worker to understand at first. For example, if your client was to tell you they found their beliefs 'distressing', this would probably, on its own, give you relatively few places to go next. One would need to establish what 'distressing' means to the individual, what other experiences may engender this same feeling, and what sort of things they do when they feel that way.

It is to this end that in the early stages of client work it may be as well to do as little 'steering' of the session as possible. CBT for these types of problems is a lengthier process than with almost any other client group and assessment is not a first session process; often it may last for as many as six to eight sessions. Throughout that process it is important to maintain an awareness of the differing aspects of the client's experience, the antecedents of unusual experiences or beliefs and the consequences of them for the individual being paramount (see formulating distressing beliefs below). It may be the case that the client attends wishing only to talk about the current experience of the belief for them in the present. Where this occurs it is important to bear in mind that the client may have taken months to reach this version of their delusion by a process of refinement or revelation and that it may be their best way to make sense of the world around them right now. Whilst it is more important in the first instance to gain a clear sense of the area of the client's life influenced by this belief (the consequences) as well as a robust and relevant history with an emphasis on stressors in both the recent and the distant past (the antecedents) than to discuss the belief itself, where this is not possible, looking at the delusion exclusively will still produce a great deal of references to both antecedents and consequences.

At the other end of the scale, some clients may come to therapy so guarded it is difficult to elicit any mention of the beliefs for which they have been referred. When this happens it is especially important to begin by seeking to gain some understanding of what the process of therapy means to the individual with an eye to gaining a deeper insight into any relevant anxieties that may be held about the process. Where gaining any information at all is a problem, it can be useful to discuss what CBT can and cannot do for individuals with experiences termed psychotic, the rights of the individual to confidentiality and respect, and the general process of therapy within a CBT framework. In such circumstances, it may also help to draw the client out by discussing their goals, since discussing hopes for therapy may give an indication of any relevant fears.

Often one of the client's first questions may be to ask if you believe them in what they are saying. When this happens it is important to focus on the delusional belief as one possible explanation for the antecedents, emphasising that until there is a greater body of information to draw upon, it is difficult to come to firm conclusions as to the validity of the belief. In general, this shifting of focus is accepted as 'good enough', representing as it does a sea change in perspective from that of many mental health professionals. Chadwick, et al. (1996) pitch this difference as one of emphasising process over content, moving from the relative 'truth' of the belief to the circumstances preceding it or the consequences (emotional, behavioural, physical and subsequent cognitions) of the clients holding this outlook. Providing frequent feedback, validating and hopefully serving to build a workable therapeutic alliance is helpful in this regard (Grant, et al., 2004, 2008).

In essence, assessment of distressing beliefs should cover conviction (how firmly the client holds the belief), preoccupation (how much time does the client spend thinking about the belief), formation (how did the client come to hold the belief) and evidence gathering (of information both supportive and contrary to the belief). Conviction and preoccupation are both liable to fluctuate to some degree over time even in the absence of therapy and, in keeping with formation, are notoriously problematic to measure with any degree of accuracy. Many therapists will begin each session with a brief inventory of both conviction and preoccupation, whether via a semi-structured interview or informally – for example, 'Today I am *X* per cent sure my belief is true' and 'I have thought about my belief *X* times today/this week', although there is little evidence that there is any merit to this approach at present. Indeed, it may be said that the process of therapy is likely to skew measures of preoccupation as the practice of monitoring and recording belief-relevant information is generally an ongoing part of the therapeutic process.

Formation is equally thorny to accurately establish, as the client is subject to all the same information processing biases and limited recall as anyone else.

REFLECTION POINT

Why do you read the newspaper or websites you choose to read? To what extent do these media support or differ from your views on various subjects? Try to list the reasons you chose these publications to inform yourself. Does this list seem exhaustive to you?

Now consider why you vote, or do not vote. How much does your chosen political stance agree with 'your' party's manifesto? Compile another list of the reasons you selected this outlook from all the available options.

Finally consider the above alongside your faith, or absence of one. Would a list of reasons for selecting this perspective be more or less comprehensive than the preceding ones?

Any listing of the reasons that led you to any of the above choices is likely to be incomplete at best and by its very nature a subjective construction.

Looking at the process of belief formation is never an exact science based, as it is, on the client's recollections of what was happening and how they felt and acted at a time often weeks or months previously. Clearly this caveat also applies to any between-session diary work, although hopefully to a lesser extent if clients are encouraged to complete their recording as soon as possible after the events described. The reason for eliciting information surrounding case formulation is more based in a search for themes common to the individual's experience – for example, rejection, loss or isolation – than to uncover a definitive answer as to how or why they came to hold this particular belief.

Case formulation of distressing beliefs

The process of formulating any problem can be done in many ways; these can be broadly split into formulations that are more specific to the diagnosed condition (nomothetic) or to the client (idiographic). Models of a nomothetic nature abound for most diagnostic areas to cover generalised presentations and experiences of, for example, OCD, health anxiety, social phobia and so on, and in very many cases these are clinically appropriate and completely sufficient. Some models of formulation are sufficiently broad as to be considered suitable for a wide range of conditions such as the five-part model described in the previous chapter.

The five-part model is sufficiently general to be applied to any problem and is often a useful primer for other, more 'diagnosis specific' types of formulation. Whilst this model may be helpful in working with distressing beliefs, in many instances the first model used will be the cognitive

ABC model – the use of which in psychotic experiences was championed by Chadwick, et al. (1996). For many years this model had fallen out of favour in CBT circles coming, as it did, from the Rational Emotive Behaviour Therapy of Albert Ellis, and to many reflecting a harking back to the more simplistic days of Behaviour Therapy where it was widely used. However, what Chadwick and his colleagues did was to modify the work of Ellis to accommodate all cognitive processes within the B column (see Tables 6.1 and 6.2), the reasons for which will be discussed later.

Table 6.1

Activating event	Beliefs (all cognitive activity relating to A: thoughts, imagery)	Consequences (emotional, behavioural, physical)

Table 6.2

Activating event	Beliefs (all cognitive activity relating to A: thoughts, imagery)	Consequences (emotional, behavioural, physical)
'Nurse walks past my room without stopping or acknowledging me.'	'She thinks she's better than me' – *Inference*	Anger
	'She's trying to keep me down' – *Evaluation*	Avoidance
		Disappointment
	Nurse laughing with colleagues in ward office – *Imagery*	Disengagement from nursing staff

As has already been noted above, the processes that may be eligible for inclusion in column B are many, and often fleeting, so to expand on this let's return to our previous example.

The ABC model serves to tease apart these differing elements of cognition and, once identified, each is more open to scrutiny and examination of validity and utility to the individual. As CBT in this area focuses on the *distressing* nature of beliefs held, there may be already preparedness on the part of the client to reconsider elements of thinking that serve to perpetuate such beliefs. However, this is not always the case and many people will only agree following a comprehensive explanation of the process of CBT to reappraise these 'B' column events. The reason for this is probably one we can all identify with: in normal conversation each day we will hear examples of people tying 'A' and 'C' together while completely side-stepping the related 'B'. Examples of this may include 'Cynthia ignored me in class today (A), I can't stand her any more' (C), or 'Because he cut me up at the traffic lights (A), I drove right on his back bumper all the way home' (C).

REFLECTION POINT

How many examples have you heard in your own life today of this sort of reasoning? How many times do you think you may have done the same? On those occasions, when you have behaved as if circumstances or others 'made' you act in that way, to what extent do you think you were aware of your own beliefs, whether global or specific to the situation whilst you were responding?

People who experience distressing beliefs share the same world and are party to the same manners of speech as anyone else, and consequently may not immediately see the impact of thoughts on the consequences of their activating experiences. In keeping with the rest of us, they are less in touch with their rules or underlying assumptions and core beliefs than they are with their inferences, imagery and evaluations. Groundwork done in the early sessions, explaining the way the ABC model works and reiterating the linear ABC process in as many examples as can be generated, will greatly assist in internalising the process of the model and with therapy in general. As with each stage, regular checking of understanding is essential.

It would require an unusually stolid client to continue to attend therapy where he was repeatedly shown real-life examples of a process that had been ineffectively explained in the first place. The best way to ensure a comprehensive understanding is to seek to elicit an explanation of how the model works (or any other relevant psychotherapeutic tool for that matter) from the clients themselves. Clearly this must be done in a sensitive manner as some people will fear 'getting it wrong' or being judged. In order to minimise the possibility of this happening, any such approach must have been outlined in as many differing ways as appropriate beforehand. Verbal explanations can be supplemented by handouts, whiteboard work in session and between-session work. The client's explanation should be judged by the yardstick of what is necessary to ensure a working understanding of the process at hand. Anything beyond this, while it may be helpful, may equally serve to confuse or misdirect the client. Ensuring client understanding of the ABC model is especially important as it serves as a microcosm of the entire CBT perspective; things happen to us (A) and what we think about them (B) leads us to act in the ways we do (C).

Very often it is necessary to 'chain' these formulations together to establish a fuller picture of the whole process of events as we shall discover below in the case of 'Paul' (see Interventions).

CASE STUDY

Paul

Throughout the discussion of interventions we will return to the experiences of 'Paul', a 28-year-old man with an 11-year history of schizophrenia.

Paul began smoking cannabis when he was 14 and, based on clinical notes, his recounting of his history and information from his mother (the only non-professional currently in regular contact with him), he became increasingly suspicious and detached from his peers from the age of 16. Paul has previously put his increased suspicion down to the fact that at that age he began dealing in cannabis in order to supplement his own intake. Interestingly about eight months prior to Paul's first hospitalisation, where he was detained under the Mental Health Act, he stated he stopped smoking cannabis, cutting off all ties with those friends with whom he had previously smoked and began training in preparation to join the Army Air Corp. It was at Paul's final interview prior to basic training that concerns were first seriously flagged up about his mental health as he spoke of his ability to 'fight without fighting' and alluded to being able to constantly stay in touch with his commanding officers and infer their orders as they thought them.

Paul has been detained in hospital on eight different occasions and has been arrested at least as many times, typically under section 136 of the Mental Health Act, and has had convictions for possession of cannabis and shoplifting in his late teens. He is thought to still smoke cannabis at least occasionally by both his mother and his community team, but generally denies this. Paul lives alone in a bed-sit across town from his mother. Following discharge from hospital four months ago, Paul was referred for CBT at his Community Mental Health Centre.

Interventions

There are a number of possible interventions at the disposal of the worker using CBT when helping someone with worrying beliefs. Regardless of the specific intervention, all work from the same common tenets insofar as they, having established a problem area to begin work on, will:

- establish the 'short-circuited' Antecedent leading directly to Consequence connection (outlined above in 'formulating distressing beliefs') as the crux of the client's problems;
- validate the emotional and behavioural Consequences;
- introduce the possibility that a change at 'B' could have affected both the Consequences and the subsequent chained ABC formulations of problems;
- discuss the specific inferential Beliefs attached to the agreed problem at hand;
- examine thematic evaluative beliefs (where appropriate) underlying the current inferred 'B';
- apply this to a formulation including developmental data (core beliefs/rules or underlying assumptions/automatic thoughts);
- test the validity and utility of the current inferred beliefs.

To expand upon these stages we shall examine each in turn.

Antecedent > consequence

In keeping with the rest of us, clients will tend to see the consequence of distressing trigger events as the true problem in almost all cases. Maintaining a focus upon the difficulties inherent in the antecedent and experienced as a result of the consequences for them serves to engage the client in the process and increase the potential for active collaboration.

Emotional and behavioural consequences

Acknowledging the difficulties caused by the consequences to the client's life again will serve to cement engagement and collaboration but more importantly sets up a possibility of change focus. To return to our last example, 'It must have been awful for you to feel so scared that you were being watched you felt you had to search your entire flat. It seems this has left your flat in disrepair and you on bad terms with your landlord and the other tenants.'

Changing Bs changes Cs

This can be the thorniest area of intervening for change to establish, yet need not be. Often generic CBT techniques can be employed to reinforce the concept that differing beliefs lead to differing consequences. Table 6.3 illustrates this by using a common antecedent leading to different consequences.

Table 6.3

Antecedent	Beliefs	Consequences
Lying in bed asleep alone at 2 a.m. you hear a noise downstairs		Fear, try to phone the police
		Anger, try to go back to sleep
		Elation, run downstairs

Clearly these are by no means the only three responses that could be elicited to this trigger.

What beliefs could underlie these wildly differing responses?

How might your actions change to this particular antecedent at differing times?

Discussions around subject matter such as the above ABC model can establish the idea that shifts in appraisal directly alter outcomes. This tends to lead naturally on to discussions of the beliefs surrounding the agreed problem area.

Problem specific inferential beliefs

All the preceding interventions are, to an extent, a preamble to gaining access to the client's own beliefs attached to the agreed problem. Very often these beliefs will be intimately tied to underlying evaluations (see below) and the therapist would be well advised to be vigilant for material of this nature arising from discussions of specific problem-related beliefs. Here is where previously mentioned ABC formulation chaining may gain the greatest results. To expand on this let's return to our client Paul. A question such as 'What was the first thing you thought when the postman knocked on the door' may get things moving.

Well the first thing I thought I guess was, 'that sounds official, and don't answer it'. Then I checked the spy-hole in the door and saw it was a bloke dressed as a postman. I walked into the kitchen and thought this must mean I was being monitored; you know that there were people interested in my activities. Then I started to wonder whether they'd known I was in at that time. I was feeling really scared now, but angry too. Just as I was thinking that I heard a car pull away outside really fast. I'm patriotic you know? I was in the army before I went into hospital the first time, signed my life over to Queen and country; proud of it too. So I couldn't figure out why they wanted me so badly.

Anyway, I thought they'd probably known I was home so I guessed they must be watching me inside my house! I knew from the TV what sort of places you'd want to hide a camera to watch a room so I started looking around. When I didn't find anything where I first looked I started to check other places, and the more I looked the more desperate I felt I guess. After a while there was another knock on the door and, when I checked, it was the woman from downstairs with the landlord. He says I have to pay for the repairs to the walls which there's no way I can afford on my benefits.

The client responds that the knock 'sounded official'. This is an inference; looking at this client's history we may see numerous 'flash-points' of conflict with perceived authority figures in the past, so in light of this the subsequent evaluation to avoid opening the door is, perhaps, understandable. Following on from this the client thought 'this means there's people interested in my activities'. Again, this appears to be inferential and may also provide the first clue to underlying evaluative thematic beliefs which we shall return to. The client expressed how this resulted in feeling fearful of being monitored and angry that he should be 'under suspicion', and his statement that he is 'a patriot' again implies evaluative beliefs about self. Following this the client again over-generalises that he is being surveyed inside his home and that this process is being done via cameras. Believing all the above and feeling anxious, desperate and angry, he proceeds to search his home. Events and experience 'chaining', such as the example above, reinforces that beliefs inform consequences which in turn skew subsequent antecedents – clearly the longer the 'chain' the greater the potential for unhelpful beliefs to cause more distressing and severe consequences as subsequent ABCs build upon the distorted beliefs of previous models (Table 6.4).

Table 6.4

Antecedent (A)	Belief (B)	Consequence (C)	A	B	C	A	B	C
Hears a knock at the door	'that sounds official', 'better not answer'	Checks front door spyhole, sees postman Increasing anxiety Increasing heart rate	*When chaining ABCs the 'C' becomes the next 'A' (i.e. check front door spyhole, see postman)*	'This must mean I'm being monitored', 'People are interested in my activities', 'how did they know I was at home'	Fear Anger Anxiety	Fear Anger Hear a car pull away quickly outside	'Why would they want me so badly?' 'They must be watching me inside my home.'	Confusion Fear Anger Sense of injustice

Evaluative thematic beliefs

The dialogue that the chained example in Table 6.4 is based on outlines some thematic beliefs about the client's perspective of himself (a 'patriot', prepared to fight for his country) and how, within his world view, he does not *deserve* to be persecuted in this way by those 'people interested in (his) activities'.

The comments regarding others imply beliefs about their perceived trustworthiness; the 'official sounding' knock at the door, the man *dressed as* a postman and how 'this *must* mean [he] was being monitored'. Returning again to the client's previous experiences contact with, as he sees them, 'figures of authority' has almost without exception resulted in perceived poor outcomes for Paul. Examples of these poor outcomes have included compulsory treatment under the Mental Health Act and being arrested. Further discussions around this subject matter elicited Paul's beliefs that others are intrusive, hostile, 'always at my door' and 'better than me'.

Expanded formulation

Subsequent to Paul's candid explanation of his experiences, as he perceives them, it becomes more understandable, though no more reasonable, to see why he would act as he did. Others are, Paul believes, more able than he. They are capable of acting in ways and for reasons he believes to be only partially understandable to him in the moment, and this belief is understandably anxiety provoking. Paul feels wronged by others and undeserving of such treatment as he does not see himself as a criminal, but feels he is being treated *as if* he were one.

A typical expanded formulation would take the lessons we have learnt from the ABC formulations and our discussions around them, what we know of Paul's history and how he sees the world, and collaboratively put these items within a framework. Below is an example of such a framework, as it would relate to Paul. This format is often termed a linear formulation.

Devising any formulation should always be a collaborative experience. The therapist (initially at least) holds the tools which will inform the structure of the model, but it is the client who is the sole arbiter of whether the model is useful, helpful or relevant. Without constant input from the client the formulation is of little use, but if both parties consider formulations to be constantly

---

PAUL'S (ABRIDGED) LINEAR FORMULATION

Relevant early experiences
- *Only child, mum 'loving but overprotective of me'.*
- *Regularly bullied up to Year 9 of school.*
- *Subsequent problems with behaviour at school, 'I became a bully when I found out how to use my fists'.*
- *'Always felt like the outsider', 'always feeling different to the other kids'.*

Core beliefs
- *I am . . . not good enough.*
- *Others are . . . untrustworthy, unpredictable, critical.*
- *The world is . . . dangerous, unjust.*

Rules/Conditional beliefs/Unhelpful assumptions
- *If others see the real me they will reject me.*
- *I should be free to be left alone at all times.*

evolving 'best guesses' or hypotheses as to how problems are activated and play out for the client at present then this perspective may serve to foster a sense of optimism as the formulation clearly outlines how changing any aspect of it will affect all subsequent parts.

Continued practice at this process will sharpen the mental health worker's sense of how a formulation 'hangs together'. There is a constant interplay between all the parts with each core belief influencing all the other ones and, in turn, the rules designed to support them. By way of, a fairly extreme, example consider the following formulation.

Core beliefs
- *I am good enough.*

- *Others are kind, decent, and benign.*

Rules/Underlying assumptions
- *I must always give 100 per cent to avoid total failure.*

- *If I can achieve it, it must be easy/worthless.*

REFLECTION EXERCISE

Take a few moments to consider this brief sketch of a formulation; does it make sense to you?

If not, what are your concerns with it?

Which would you be more inclined to see as the more accurate illustration of the how things are at present for this client: the 'rules' or the core beliefs?

Perhaps the most prudent answer to the last of the above questions would be achieved by discussing this mismatch with the client. By asking the client how they see the above assertions fitting together we can minimise the likelihood of trying to make the formulation 'work' at the expense of maintaining accuracy. An accurate formulation cannot help but 'work' as it is merely a simplified pictorial version of the way that the client functions.

There may be times where it is not possible to draw up an expanded formulation shoulder-to-shoulder with the client and one has to be drafted outside the session and brought in to be reviewed by the client. Where this is the only practical manner in which to draft a formulation, as much time as is needed should be given to the client to reflect and feedback on its content. The mental health worker should be especially cautious to gain as much feedback as possible where the preliminary formulation would appear to indicate dependency, low self-esteem or other traits that may make it difficult for the client to feel able to give a full, honest and open appraisal of the validity of the formulation. At such times it may be helpful to explore alternative ways of giving feedback or other interventions to maximise client involvement.

Test the validity and utility of the current inferred beliefs

Once you and your client have agreed on all the above, and assuming your client is open to changing his beliefs (this needs to be explicitly checked out with the client), the next stage must be to decide upon a goal to work practically upon and, having done so, agree upon the steps needed to achieve it. Establishing a clear, realistic goal pitched to the right stage in the therapy process (i.e. achievable but still challenging), that can be measured by a predetermined method within a specific time frame, is an essential aspect of any CB intervention. The above sentence paraphrases the somewhat hackneyed SMART (see below) mnemonic; however, it is important to remember that in therapy goal setting will often flow naturally out of initial assessment as the client outlines their primary concerns.

- **S**pecific

- **M**easurable

- **A**chievable

- **R**ealistic

- **T**ime limited

Consequently, sentences such as 'The main thing that worries me is X' or 'I'd be fine if only X was different' can quickly lead to a mutually agreeable defined problem area which will in turn inform the goal. Once a goal is clearly defined and understood within the context of the preceding stages, discussion will generally move naturally towards methods of achieving the stated aim. There are many ways to approach this, and this process has an inevitable knock-on effect upon the individual's rules, and this phenomenon may be subsequently revisited and more adaptive, client-generated, rules devised.

Identified goals and, as in all preceding areas of the therapeutic process, any such plans must be a collaborative endeavour. Lastly, it should be borne in mind that clients who do not feel a sense of ownership of therapy goals are much less likely to progress in therapy in general. We can illustrate the goal-setting process using an example from Paul's therapy.

CASE STUDY

Throughout early sessions of therapy, Paul made numerous references to 'officials' being 'always at my door'. Paul was highly motivated to tackle this difficulty so we agreed to look into this area in greater detail. Paul expressed a goal of seeking to reduce his stress when in contact with officials. Consequently, finding out exactly what 'officials' meant to Paul was our starting point.

Paul's initial definition of officials included (but was not limited to) emergency services, social services, community mental health workers, postmen, milkmen, his landlord, workmen and his neighbours. When the full list was given to Paul for review he laughed and remarked 'That's pretty much everyone who's been to my door in the last five years apart from my mum'.

At times of acute illness, entry had been twice forced to Paul's flat by the police under the Mental Health Act. Paul disclosed he often 'saw' this process happening again when someone knocked on his door. Imagery such as this triggered feelings of fear and anger, and consequently he would often avoid opening the door. Following work on managing the impact of this sort of imagery, we revisited the above linear formulation, looking specifically at Paul's beliefs and rules about others and he acknowledged that these beliefs may play a part in responding as he does. Returning to the list of 'officials' we discussed whether, on the occasions Paul did answer the door, these people were all equally difficult to interact with. Paul felt they were not, citing the police, his landlord and social workers as 'the real officials' at this time. This revision led to two separate lists: 'officials' and 'other people who come to my door'. Role play led to a better understanding of exactly how Paul would respond when he did open the door, and this was typified by poor, or no, eye contact, clipped speech and rapid breathing.

CASE STUDY *continued*

I fed back to Paul that his role-play responses, were I a stranger at his door, would probably have left me feeling frightened and equally as keen to leave as he was to close the door. Paul was surprised at this and disclosed that he thought I was exaggerating. After we agreed I role-play these responses to Paul, he acknowledged this approach may seem intimidating to others. Paul was reminded that in almost all situations he retained the right to just shut his door if he felt overwhelmed. Discussions around how we could modify behaviours naturally led to testing out how differing responses may influence our interactions with others. Paul felt that some expressions or responses just weren't suitable for him and would feel false and probably serve to increase his anxiety. However, by maintaining an open and curious discussion with frequent brief role plays, he decided that whilst acknowledging the anxiety triggered by others at his door he could test out at home a formula of keeping conversations brief and purposeful, paying attention to the depth and pace of his breathing and giving limited eye contact. Potential problems were discussed and Paul suggested putting a note on the back of his door to remind him of the experiment. Beyond this, we discussed how previous experiences of others of knocking at his door may colour their responses to Paul's experiment regardless of his present responses and how sometimes, despite our best efforts, others may still be rude or abrupt. We went on to discuss how Paul would manage such responses.

In line with Paul's goal, we agreed that his stress in such interactions would be subjectively measured on a one to ten scale and that he would keep a brief diary of who called and the reason why and stress levels prior to opening the door and during the conversation. This was to be reviewed at our next meeting.

Following such experiments and evidence gathering of outcomes, therapy can begin to discuss the usefulness of holding such beliefs. When the client acknowledges that beliefs are the cause of problematic consequences and is prepared to experiment with alternative perspectives to their present outlook (however tentatively), it is essential to seek to review and compare experimental outcomes to the predictions inherent within previously expressed beliefs in sufficient detail to highlight any discrepancies. However, it is important to observe any inconsistencies in a sensitive manner. Our beliefs are a large part of what makes us who we are and it is easy for excessive challenges to be seen as an attack upon the client. Crucially, the client must be allowed to seek alternative explanations to any inconsistencies without being 'led' towards any particular viewpoint by the therapist. Subsequent hypotheses may be tested in a similar manner.

C H A P T E R   S U M M A R Y

CBT for distressing and false beliefs can be a valuable tool to improve quality of life, raise self-esteem and reduce the possibility of relapse. There are, however, unique challenges for mental health workers using CBT with this client group. Attaining effective engagement and collaboration in the process of therapy may take many months. It is also the case that therapeutic alliance ruptures which are unattended to may rapidly lead to the discontinuation of therapy.

The pace of change may be extremely slow at times, and lengthy periods may be spent maintaining the client–therapist bond as are spent working on the problems that brought the client into CBT in the first place. Finally, the interventions outlined above are no more than a brief sketch of those aspects of the process of therapy upon which greater emphasis is placed when working with this specific client group.

CAVEAT ABOUT CBT FOR THE ISSUES OUTLINED IN THIS CHAPTER

High-intensity practitioners (trained under the recent 'Improving Access to Psychological Therapies' initiative) will not be working with clients to resolve issues such as the ones outlined in this chapter. Consequently, any work undertaken with these problems, in common with any other CBT practice, must take place against a background of further training, informed practice and appropriate CBT supervision. The types of difficulties outlined in this chapter are often made more difficult by other aspects of the presentation of those individuals who experience such distressing perceptions and thoughts.

An awareness of the techniques used to help people suffering from distressing appraisals of their 'psychotic' experiences is not the same as a proficiency in resolving such problems.

FURTHER READING

Bentall, RP (2004) *Madness explained: Psychosis and human nature.* London: Penguin.

In this successfully ambitious work, Bentall deconstructs common modern thinking surrounding psychosis. The author argues that 'madness' cannot be defined as an illness to be cured like any other. He asserts that labels such as 'schizophrenia' and 'manic depression' are meaningless, based as they are on nineteenth-century classifications, and that experiences such as delusions and hearing voices are exaggerations of psychological experiences to which we are all vulnerable.

Chadwick P, Birchwood, M and Trower, P (1996) *Cognitive therapy for delusions, voices and paranoia.* Chichester: Wiley.

This, and the Haddock and Slade book below, are excellent texts for those wishing to work with people who hear voices.

Freeman, D, Freeman, J and Garety, P (2006) *Overcoming paranoid and suspicious thoughts: A self help guide using cognitive behavioural techniques.* London: Robinson.

As the title of this book suggests, it is a (very useful) self-help text for use by those people suffering from paranoid and suspicious beliefs.

Haddock, G and Slade, PD (1996) *Cognitive–behavioural interventions with psychotic disorders.* London: Routledge.

Morrison, AP (2002) *A casebook of cognitive therapy for psychosis.* Hove: Brunner-Routledge.

This book provides excellent coverage of a variety of casebook material.

Morrison, AP, Renton, J, French, P and Bentall, R (2008) *Think you're crazy? Think again: A resource book for cognitive therapy for psychosis.* London: Routledge.

Perhaps inevitably because of the difficulty and very slow pace of working with this client group, CB therapists need to be resilient and creative. In this context, this book should prove to be enormously helpful.

USEFUL WEBSITES

www.comingoff.com

This website was developed by Rufus May, clinical psychologist and advocate for those who suffer from distressing beliefs and hear voices, and his colleagues. It is a useful resource for clients and mental health workers who want to explore the safe withdrawal from psychotrophic medication in conjunction with other approaches.

Chapter 7

Helping people with Borderline Personality Disorder

Alec Grant

C H A P T E R   A I M S

After reading this chapter you will be able to:

- understand the significance of the phrase 'diagnosis of social exclusion', when used in relation to personality disorder;

- have some awareness of the growing evidence base for psychological therapy for personality disorder generally and Borderline Personality Disorder specifically;

- know the inclusion criteria for placing someone in the diagnostic category of Borderline Personality Disorder;

- be able to describe the main reasons why a person might have Borderline Personality Disorder in adulthood;

- outline the cognitive model of personality disorder;

- describe the general CBT principles, and specific cognitive and behavioural strategies, for helping Borderline clients;

- understand the importance and significance of the therapeutic relationship in working with Borderline clients.

Introduction

Unfortunately, it has historically been the case, and continues to be so in some areas, that the term 'personality disorder', subsuming Borderline Personality Disorder, is used as a 'diagnosis of social exclusion' in mainstream mental health services (Castillo, et al., 2001; Eastwick and Grant 2005; Mills, et al., 2004b). As will be seen as this chapter unfolds, this seems ironic given that mental health practitioners, while rallying against the causes of childhood abuse and neglect, are less willing to understand or engage with the longer-term consequences of it in practice. It is a sad state of affairs that Borderline clients' understandable, but maladaptive, responses tend to be negatively evaluated by mental health workers. Indeed, the term 'Borderline Personality Disorder' is often used to make moral, as opposed to professional, interpretations of clients' behaviour, by labelling it as inappropriate, manipulative and disruptive. Such labelling absolves mental health workers from the professional responsibility to understand and contextualise such behaviour, and from investing in the kinds of therapeutic alliances and helping processes that will be described in this chapter.

> *ACTIVITY 7.1*
>
> Discuss what feelings the term 'personality disorder' evokes in you. Do you know anyone who has been given this diagnostic label?

> *REFLECTION POINT*
>
> Looking back over your life, have there been any protracted periods of time when your thoughts and your behaviour have been driven by strong emotions?

> *RESEARCH SUMMARY*
>
> The psychological treatment for personality disorders has developed and improved in the last two decades. There now exists a good evidence base to support the view that a lot can be done to help those suffering from personality disorders reduce their distress and their serious behavioural problems. Indeed, Silk (2008) argues that, compared with pharmacological treatments, psychological treatments have been much more promising. This seems particularly to be the case for Borderline Personality Disorder as there have been more randomised controlled trials of psychological treatments carried out for this form of personality disorder than for any other.
>
> *(Duggan, et al., 2007)*
>
> *Individuals with Borderline Personality Disorder are highly likely to seek out and receive help from health services. It is also the case that the distinct pattern of problems, including high suicide rates, makes the diagnosis of Borderline Personality Disorder more recognisable to mental health professionals. All of this has contributed to more research being conducted to improve psychological treatments for those suffering from the disorder.*

Diagnosis

The diagnosis of Borderline Personality Disorder is a relatively new one, appearing first in the American Psychiatric Association's *(DSM-III)* in 1980. In terms of both American and world diagnostic systems, the diagnostic criteria for BPD include pervasive and unstable interpersonal relationships and self-image, and marked impulsivity (APA, 2000; WHO, 1992). This is said to begin by early adulthood and appear evident across different contexts in the client's life. To meet the diagnostic criteria, at least five of the following nine criteria have to be in evidence: fear of abandonment; unstable and intense personal relationships; identity disturbance; impulsivity; recurrent deliberate self-harm; unstable affect; feeling of emptiness; difficulties controlling anger; and stress-related paranoid ideas or dissociation.

The DSM-IV also states that clients experience an intense fear of abandonment. Actual or feared abandonment is, in turn, linked to the Borderline Personality Disordered clients' views of their self-worth (Beck, et al., 1990), and clients will take extraordinary measures to prevent real or imagined rejection or abandonment (Eastwick and Grant, 2005).

With regard to impulsivity, Borderline clients display a marked tendency to act impulsively without considering the consequences of impulsive actions. In relation to this, they also exhibit an inability to plan ahead. Lacking self-control, they display outbursts of intense anger. This can result in violence and other extreme behaviours, and this seems to be especially the case if the Borderline client's impulsive acts are challenged or prevented by the people around them.

CBT for Borderline Personality Disorder

CBT has been demonstrated to be an effective psychological treatment for Borderline Personality Disorder (Davidson, et al., 2006). Forms of cognitive psychotherapy which are more explicitly focused on working at the level of the client's core beliefs, or schemas, have also been seen to be effective in treating Borderline Personality Disorder (Young, et al., 2003; Giesen-Bloo, et al., 2006). So-called schema-focused therapy is delivered over three years, twice weekly. This contrasts with the more standard form of CBT for Personality Disorders (CBTpd), championed by Davidson and her colleagues (Davidson, et al., 2006), which consists of 30 sessions delivered over one year.

Can we be hopeful of change?

Traditionally, personality disorder was view as an unchangeable condition. It is not surprising that pessimistic views about change, with or without formal treatment, prevailed. However, it is currently the case that the prognosis or outcome, at least for personality disorder, is better than was originally thought to be the case (Skodol, et al., 2005). However, it must be borne in mind that after 27 years the death rate attributable to suicide can be as high as 10 per cent (Paris and Zweig-Frank, 2001). Long-term follow-up research on people with a diagnosis of Borderline Personality Disorder suggests that around half of them will no longer meet the diagnostic criteria for the disorder at the five-year point, and that this percentage continues to increase over time (Zanarini, et al., 2003). However, this picture does not imply that individuals diagnosed with Borderline Personality Disorder are free from problems when they no longer meet the diagnostic criteria. It seems to be the case that certain problems change little, such as disturbance in affect and impulsiveness, while behavioural problems such as self-harm change more.

Borderline Personality Disorder as a developmental problem?

Taking a diagnostic view of Borderline Personality Disorder is extremely useful. However, psychological formulations of the problem area can complement and challenge a diagnostic standpoint. Whereas the diagnostic approach, generally, tends to represent people in 'disordered' terms, psychological formulations suggest a different picture – one of individuals whose problems are understandable given the context of their disadvantaged developmental backgrounds.

Linehan (1987) argues that the reason Borderline clients have difficulty regulating their emotions and their impulses is because of the experiences they had while growing up: specifically, the repeated experiences of having their emotional reactions trivialised or discounted by significant others in their lives. From this perspective, these invalidating social environments result in people who have failed to develop the necessary skills of emotional regulation.

An additional, but related, problem is that because their emotional communication is constantly and consistently invalidated, individuals who go on to develop Borderline problems come to believe that they are expected to solve difficulties arising in their lives without having the personal resources to do this. By default, this leaves them with two polarised possibilities for achieving self-affirmation: either dramatic outbursts of emotion or avoidance of people and maladaptive ways of emotional and cognitive self-management.

The cognitive model of personality disorder

It seems certainly the case that the identity of adults, in terms of the kinds of relationships that they develop, and their emotional and behavioural responses, are shaped by early attachments to (significant other) caregivers. This results in an 'inner working model' of interpersonal relationships. The histories of many Borderline clients suggest that they have been abused, and/or neglected and treated in an inconsistent manner by their childhood caregivers.

However, not all people who have the above childhood experiences go on to develop personality disorders or related problems. Rutter (1993) argues that it could be the case that Borderline clients have more frequent, extreme or enduring negative experiences, as well as temperamental dispositions which make them more vulnerable to being adversely effected by negative life experiences. According to Rutter, Borderline clients may also learn and develop less active strategies in seeking the kinds of adaptive relationships that may counteract such negative experiences.

Arguably, viewing personality disorders *solely* as developmental problems may be too simplistic. The cognitive model of personality disorder stresses the role of cognitive, emotional and behavioural aspects in the development and maintenance of such problems. It is not really clear how personality disorders arise. However, from the research to date, there are many psychological, biological and social factors which are regarded as contributing towards the probability that personality disorder will develop. In short, the origins of personality disorders are likely to be multifactorial. The cognitive model must therefore take account of:

- the inherent temperament of the child;
- genetic factors;
- childhood development and experience;
- attachment to significant others in childhood.

With the above factors in mind, Davidson (2007) argues that a model of personality disorder should be multifaceted. Child development occurs in the context of continual changes in physiological, biological, behavioural, cognitive, social and emotional structures. All of these occur in family, social and broader cultural systems.

General CBT principles in helping Borderline clients

An overarching principle in working with Borderline clients is helping them understand how their childhood development and background relates to the difficulties they experience in adulthood, which brings them into therapy (Davidson, et al., 2010). According to Davidson and her colleagues, the development of a case formulation with a Borderline client must take a considerably greater perspective on the client's early experiences and their temperament than would be the case when working with a client without a personality disorder. A detailed personal, relationship and family history gives crucial information to workers using the CB approach about the client's early experiences and relationships with key caregivers in their lives. The development of such a historical account is inevitably likely to be worked on over several sessions, in order for the mental health worker to glean a good understanding of their client's developmental and formative experiences.

A useful next step is to reflect the client's problems back to them in a letter (Davidson, et al., 2010). The ways in which clients developed the beliefs that they hold about themselves and others should be clear in such a letter, which needs to be agreed by the client and, thus, may take several drafts. It should also explain how they came to over-develop certain problematic behaviours. It is likely that such behaviours made sense in terms of their role as coping strategies for the Borderline client in early childhood, and currently make sense in relation to their beliefs about self and others. In essence, these behaviours were adaptive in childhood, becoming maladaptive in adulthood.

In keeping with the emotion, thought, behaviour linkage characteristic of CBT (Grant, et al., 2008), it is important to clarify the maladaptive core beliefs the client holds, and to identify how these relate to negative mood and to overdeveloped behavioural patterns which prevent the client from acting in an adaptive manner, especially with others. The CB intervention will target such beliefs, developed from childhood onwards, along with their associated coping behaviours.

The therapeutic relationship

It may be obvious at this stage that the client's long-held beliefs about self and others may well have a negative impact on the therapeutic relationship with the mental health worker. The Borderline client is likely to have poor self-esteem and to over-react to perceived criticism. Although they will have to work hard to achieve this, the mental health worker can use the therapeutic relationship as a 'social laboratory' to facilitate the development of both new interpersonally related beliefs and behaviours and new understandings of the client's self/in relation to others. All this will take much more time and effort compared with the practice of CBT with clients who do not have personality disorders.

Cognitive and behavioural strategies

Cognitive strategies

As a general style of dialogue, Socratic questioning is important in all CB work. However, its use is especially important in work with Borderline clients in relation to helping them generate alternative beliefs about others' thoughts and behaviour (Mills, et al., 2004b). It may also be useful to employ the continuum method (see Mills, et al., 2004b) to help the client challenge their rigidly held beliefs about self and others.

Another important cognitive strategy is helping clients to regulate their emotions through awareness of their meaning. To facilitate this, it is useful for clients to keep a thought/emotion/behaviour diary. This strategy is helpful in enabling clients' understanding of the meanings attached to emotional disturbances and enabling them to achieve an increase in tolerance of uncertainty.

Having identified a new, adaptive belief about self in relation to others, it may be helpful for clients to keep a record of experiences which support this new belief. This is sometimes referred to in cognitive behavioural circles as a 'positive data log'.

Where possible and relevant, it is often useful to involve significant others in the client's life. Such involvement can enhance relationships that are already positive, and can help bring about change in problematic relationships.

Behavioural and mood regulation strategies

From the beginning of therapy, it is important for the worker to manage both risk and suicidal behaviour. Most, if not all, mental health services and agencies have risk management strategies at their disposal which should be used. Building on this, a useful exercise for the worker and client to carry out is a cost benefit analysis of both living and committing suicide. This is a fairly simple exercise as a cost benefit analysis is usually composed of two columns with the pros (of living, then later on a separate sheet of committing suicide) written on one column and the cons on the other column. It might also be useful to have another sheet with the pros and cons of in-patient admission, carried out in the interests of the client's safety, as well as discussing with the client any personal plans for maintaining safety.

In the overall spirit of crisis management, it is useful to develop a crisis plan for very difficult times. This can include identifying the individual friends and family members that the client could contact, and ensuring that the client knows how to access their GP and emergency mental health services.

In managing deliberate self-harm, such as self-cutting, it is useful to identify its function and the client's motives and emotions at play. Helping the client increase their self-care should result in a reduction in self-harm behaviours. This could include helping the client develop more adaptive behaviours to reduce distressing emotions.

Aggressive feelings and related behaviours can be reduced by helping the client develop self-assertion skills, and by the use of simple 'stop and think' strategies. There may be other factors at play that could be addressed, including excess alcohol consumption.

Mood management may be developed through the use of several strategies. Simple distraction technique can be utilised, as can the use of meditation techniques. Mindfulness meditation is currently in vogue in CBT practice (see e.g. Williams, et al., 2007) and is simple to learn. Finally, if clients are capable of this, it is helpful to encourage them to develop a strategy of knowing that the distressing mood will pass.

Finally, helping clients take better care of themselves may be achieved by simple behavioural experiments (Grant, et al., 2004, 2008). These could be built on identifying the factors and behaviours at play in poor self-care. It may, for example, be useful for clients to see the effects on their mood by eating regularly or getting more sleep.

Case study: Karen

Karen is a 25-year-old woman, referred for CBT. She was seen on a weekly basis as an outpatient. From assessment, which was undertaken over several sessions, it was clear that Karen had poor self-esteem, feared abandonment, was very impulsive, felt 'empty inside', felt very angry a lot of the time and acted on this, and cut her arms when she experienced very strong emotions. She also reported intense, volatile and unstable relationships with friends and with numerous boyfriends. It was considered by both Karen and her CB therapist that her risk of attempting suicide was low.

At a very early stage in therapy, the mental health worker discussed with Karen the very high probability that the thoughts and behaviours constituting her problem in her day-to-day life would be played out in the therapy sessions. Karen agreed that this was likely to be the case. The worker was very reassuring on this point, stressing that the therapy sessions were a kind of 'social laboratory' where dysfunctional thinking and behaviours could be readily identified and new, more functional, thinking and behaviour could be identified and tested out, and consolidated, in real life. This notion made a lot of sense to Karen, and she was very encouraged by it.

The assessment process addressed her personal, relational and family history in detail and it became apparent that Karen grew up with very dysfunctional caregivers. From her self-report, her father was absent most of the time. Her mother often ignored her, especially when Karen was distressed, and could be very inconsistent in her responses – sometimes screaming aggressively at Karen, sometimes locking her in the cellar, and at other times ignoring her, often for days on end. Karen grew up with few friends, spending long periods on her own.

As described above, her adult relationships were volatile and characterised by a series of crises, often provoked by her. She would jump from being over 'clingy' to picking arguments with friends and boyfriends alike, in response to real or imagined slights, to avoidance of friends and boyfriends when she would isolate herself. She was also frequently violent towards her current boyfriend, as she had been to previous ones. She presented for help, partly through her own volition and partly because her current boyfriend had threatened to end the relationship if she did not seek help (it should be noted at this point that he was unwilling to take part in therapy).

During the assessment session, Karen's maladaptive schema (or core beliefs) and related rules for living were identified (Pretzer, 1990; Young, 1990). These are described in Table 7.1, and made sense to Karen in terms of her upbringing, and personal, relational and family history.

Table 7.1 Karen's maladaptive schemas and related rules for living

Early maladaptive schema	Related rule for living
Abandonment/loss	'If I don't take steps to prevent this, I will be alone forever and nobody will be there for me'. (Rule 1)
Unloveability	'If people really got to know me, they would not love me. Nor would they want to be close to me'. (Rule 2)
Dependence	'If I'm on my own, then I won't be able to cope'. (Rule 3)
Subjugation/lack of individuation	'Unless I subjugate my wants and needs to the desires of others, I'll be abandoned or abused by them'. (Rule 4)
Mistrust	'If I don't protect myself, people will take advantage of me or hurt me'. (Rule 5)
Inadequate self-discipline	'Because I can't control or discipline myself, I must be reliant on others'. (Rule 6)
Fear of losing emotional control	'If I don't take steps to control my emotions, something terrible will happen'. (Rule 7)
Guilt/punishment	'I deserve to be punished because I am a bad person'. (Rule 8)
Emotional deprivation	'Because I do not believe there is anyone who can meet my needs or be strong and care for me, I must constantly be on the look-out for emotional support'. (Rule 9)

ACTIVITY 7.2

Think about the relationship between Karen's rules for living and her early upbringing at the hands of her (mostly) mother. Imagine each of you were growing up in similar circumstances. In what ways might the above rules for living have been functional in your early life? Or, to put it another way, how might living according to these rules have protected you?

ACTIVITY 7.3

Have a guess at what emotions (moods) and behaviours might go with the above rules for living.

After identifying the early experiences, at the hands of her mother, that were likely to have led to Karen's maladaptive schemas or core beliefs, and corresponding rules for living, the assessment process moved to the 'here and now' to look at examples of the relationship between her day-to-day thinking, her moods and her behaviours, illustrated in Table 7.2. Note the relationship between her everyday, sometimes called 'automatic', thinking and her rules for living (the latter put in brackets according to its number (in Table 7.1)).

Table 7.2 Thoughts, moods, behaviours

Karen's day to day thinking	Her related moods	Her related behaviour/s
My boyfriend's not paying as much attention to me as before. This must mean he's losing interest in me and will leave me. (Rule 1)	Fear Depression	Extreme clinginess towards boyfriend. Anticipation of the kind of woman he wants her to be and acting in this way, even if it means subjugating her own needs and values.
I gave away too much about myself to Ruth (friend) the other day. (Rule 2)	Fear	Avoids meeting with Ruth for two months.
Pre-occupation with the fact that my boyfriend is going away on a business trip for a month. (Rule 3)	Fear	Making arrangements for a close friend to stay with her for the period that her boyfriend is away.
I must be the kind of friend/lover that I think my friends want me to be. (Rule 4)	Anxiety	Covert attempts made to figure out what her girlfriends value in a friend and what her boyfriend values in a partner. After having found these things out, trying to change her personality and behaviour accordingly.
My boyfriend doesn't really care for me; he just wants to use me. (Rule 5)	Anger	Gets drunk and screams abuse at boyfriend, then attacks him, slapping and scratching at his face.
I can't be bothered to do the weekly shopping. I'll only screw it up and get the wrong things. (Rule 6)	Lethargy Low mood Anxiety	Asks boyfriend to do it.
I can't stand this; I'm getting more and more wound up. (Rule 7)	Extreme fear	Cuts the inside of her forearms for 10 minutes, in secret.
I'm useless; I'm no good; I deserve everything I get. (Rule 8)	Slightly depressed 'Flat'	Saying 'sorry' over-frequently to boyfriend and friends. Agreeing with their put-downs of her.
I'm really not getting the level of support I need from my friends and boyfriend. (Rule 9)	Anxiety	Trying to cultivate new friendship constantly, often at work, and then behaving in a clingy way in these relationships.

Therapy for Karen

The above information, all gleaned during the assessment process, was formulated in a letter which was given to Karen. She agreed with its contents and, after a brief discussion with the mental health worker who was helping her, it was decided between both parties that there was no need to alter the letter in any way.

Karen was intrigued by the idea of a clear link between her early life experiences, her core beliefs and rules for living, and her day-to-day thoughts, emotions and behaviours. It felt important to her to become better able to manage her emotions. A number of strategies, some of which were described earlier, were used to help her do this. First, she kept a daily diary of thoughts, emotions (moods) and behaviours (a cross-section of which is described in Table 7.2). This diary enabled her to see important trends in her life between her thinking, moods and behaviours, and became the basis for a number of emotion-regulating behavioural experiments, described in Table 7.3. The order in which Karen agreed to run the experiments was based on her level of subjective distress associated with each behaviour.

Table 7.3 Karen's behavioural experiments

Problem behaviour	Level of distress associated with it (0–100)	Behavioural experiment	What Karen found out
Cuts the inside of her forearms for 10 minutes, in secret.	80	Gradually increase the time spent between wanting to cut and actually doing it.	Karen realised that her emotions did not spiral out of control, to the point at which she died or had a heart attack, if she did not take action by self-cutting. This enabled her to gradually abandon self-cutting as a mood regulating behaviour.
Gets drunk and screams abuse at boyfriend, then attacks him, slapping and scratching at his face.	65	After distinguishing between reasonable and unreasonable feelings of annoyance with her boyfriend, Karen agreed to assertively stand up for herself about her reasonable feelings. Self assertive dialogues were modelled and role-played in therapy sessions.	Karen was pleased to find out that she was able to have her needs met in a more satisfactory way with her boyfriend by talking things through calmly and assertively. Within two months, the frequency of violent arguments with her boyfriend reduced from once to twice a week to zero. Her ability to sort interpersonal difficulties out in an assertive manner generalised to relationships with her friends and work colleagues. In turn, this markedly reduced her clinginess, her over-apologetic behaviour and her overall ability to be more independent.

ACTIVITY **7.4**

> Go back to Table 7.2. What other thought, mood, behaviour difficulties might have been improved as a result of the experiments described in Table 7.3. What other possible behavioural experiments might have been useful given the difficulties described in Table 7.2?

Post-experiment positive data logs

It is clear from the above that behavioural experiments directed at one thought, mood and behaviour problem area can have a beneficial effect on others. In order to consolidate the improvements Karen experienced as a result of engaging in behavioural experiments, she agreed to try out keeping positive data logs based around the following new rules:

> *Because I have learned new, more positive strategies to handle my emotions (self-assertion and allowing emotions to occur, trusting that they will pass), I can use these in future when I feel strong emotion. I do not need to fall back on old, dysfunctional ways. (See old Rule 7 above.)*

> *I have strong evidence, collected over the years, that I am a likeable person. I can be open and honest with people without fear of rejection, abuse or being taken advantage of, as this is a universal human right. I can also, therefore, stand up for my own values just as everyone should, without worrying that this will cause problems for others. (See old Rules 1, 2, 4, 5 above.)*

There are good reasons why keeping a positive data log is useful, both for people with Borderline Personality Disorder and for others. Behaviour is often 'mood-congruent'. This means that certain moods tend to co-occur with related forms of thinking which, in turn, relate to dysfunctional forms of behaviour. Mood-congruent behaviour also relates to the tendency in all of us to perceive information in ways directly related to our beliefs about ourselves. So, with Karen as an example, she was in large part driven by her core belief or schema of not being loveable. Because of this, she was more likely to 'notice' things happening in her interpersonal world which confirmed that core belief. Even when neutral things happened between herself and another person – boyfriend, friend or work colleague – such as a work colleague appearing very busy, therefore not willing to spend time talking with her, she would 'skew' this information in ways that fitted her 'unloveable' core belief ('She doesn't like me'). Always on the look out for rejection and slights, she would fail to notice information from interpersonal encounters, coming in through her vision and hearing, that suggested the opposite: that she was, in fact, acceptable, likeable and loveable for some people.

Karen thus needed to practice *looking out for and noticing* information from interpersonal encounters in keeping with a new likeability rule and related core belief/s. The initial positive data log for this new core belief(s)/rule is shown in Table 7.4

Table 7.4 New core belief(s)/rule

Date	New rule	Evidence to support this new rule
	I have strong evidence, collected over the years, that I am a likeable person. I can be open and honest with people without fear of rejection, abuse or being taken advantage of, as this is a universal human right. I can also, therefore, stand up for my own values just as everyone should, without worrying that this will cause problems for others.	

By keeping this data log over several weeks, Karen found that the data she gathered clearly demonstrated that she was an acceptable person. The data gathered from encounters with her friends and boyfriend also told her that, like most people, she could be unconditionally likeable, also loveable, 'warts and all'. Keeping the log also helped her positively modify all her other schemas and related rules: she felt it less of a likelihood that she would be abandoned; she realised that she could cope and get by on her own and came to value her new independence; she also found that she could relate to others on her own terms without sacrificing her integrity; it became more evident that she did not need to take over-protective steps to avoid being hurt by others; finally, she realised that she had better control of her level of emotional arousal and that, like thoughts, emotions passed and she need not be afraid of them.

The therapeutic relationship throughout the course of therapy with Karen

At the beginning of therapy, Karen was quick to notice perceived criticism from her therapist. The latter used this as an opportunity to scrutinise the specific point at which Karen noticed her therapist being critical, and unpack the meaning(s) Karen attributed to the interpersonal event and the moods that went with it. Both then engaged in a discussion around the significance of Karen's perception of being criticised in relation to the event–mood–thought–behaviour patterns (Grant, et al., 2008) in her in interpersonal life. As time went on, and Karen engaged in behavioural experiments and later positive data log work, there was a marked reduction in such misperceptions; indeed, she was able to accept and positively respond to, at first gentle, then increasingly more robust, challenges to her beliefs and related behaviour around being with others in her life.

It was also the case that, in the early weeks of therapy, Karen was prone to exhibit periods of clinginess to the therapist, where she apparently wanted to change the nature of the therapeutic relationship to a close friendship. At first, when this was pointed out to her gently, it would evoke an aggressive response from Karen. Later, she was more able to tolerate, accept and even come to like a boundaried relationship in CB therapy.

C H A P T E R   S U M M A R Y

It is important to understand the significance of the phrase 'diagnosis of social exclusion' when attempting CBT interventions with individuals who have a diagnosis of Borderline Personality Disorder. It is also important to have an awareness of the growing evidence base for psychological therapy for personality disorder generally and Borderline Personality Disorder specifically. There are clear inclusion criteria for placing someone in the diagnostic category of Borderline Personality Disorder, and there are good developmental and social reasons why a person might have Borderline Personality Disorder in adulthood. On the basis of the cognitive model of personality disorder, general CBT principles and specific cognitive and behavioural strategies are effective in helping Borderline clients. Finally, the therapeutic relationship is crucially important and significant when working with Borderline Personality Disordered individuals.

FURTHER READING

Arntz, A and Van Gerderen, H (2009) *Schema therapy for borderline personality disorder.* Chichester: Wiley-Blackwell.

This book is a contemporary text covering detailed, case-based, schema-focused treatment techniques in a very practical way.

Davidson, K (2007) *Cognitive therapy for personality disorders: A guide for clinicians.* 2nd edition. Routledge: Hove.

This text is based on the development of standard CBT for personality disorders. It too is practical, and grounded in detailed and extensive case material.

Young, JE, Klosko, JS and Weishaar, ME (2007) *Schema therapy. A practitioner's guide.* New York: The Guilford Press.

This seminal text demonstrates how the standard cognitive therapy approaches to Axis 1 disorders can be expanded and modified to treat personality disorders. The book is based on a comprehensive cognitive model, within which a variety of strategies are drawn on to address the specific problems in this population: rigid, lifelong maladaptive characterological patterns; chronic interpersonal difficulties; and transference reactions.

USEFUL WEBSITES

www.nice.org.uk/Guidance/CG78

This site contains the British clinical guidelines for the evidence-based treatment of Borderline Personality Disorder.

www.bpdworld.org/

This is a very useful Borderline Personality Disorder support and information site, run by volunteers.

Conclusion

Alec Grant

C H A P T E R   A I M S

After reading this chapter you will be able to:

- better understand the contextual basis for the practice of CBT;
- understand the characteristics of CBT-friendly cultures;
- identify key ingredients of work-culture preparation.

CBT in context

In important respects, this book is all about the contextual understanding of CBT. It began by contextualising CBT in the history of twentieth-century applied psychology. It then addressed the fundamental principles of the cognitive model or emotional response, or the contextual importance of the role of thinking in human distress and mental health difficulties. It looked at the developmental benefits for future CBT clients and practitioners, including the cognitive context for confidence problems among therapists early in their training.

Following this, the focus shifted to the international and national healthcare and policy context for the need and delivery of CBT. This discussion touched on the national stepped care delivery context and the relevance for mental health nurse education, and educational policy. It was asserted that nurse education and policy has hitherto been characterised by resistance and an investment in custom and practice-based, as opposed to evidence-based, interventions.

The narrative then addressed the context of preparation for the first meeting with the client. It was argued that this was a crucial time in giving positive first impressions, but, based on examples from real life, may regrettably result in poor and negative experiences for the client. The steps needed to pre-empt such experiences were clearly stated.

The rudiments of assessment are also contextualised in the first, and subsequent early, meetings with the client. The products of a structured assessment, such as the one illustrated in Chapter 4, provides the contextual basis for informed CB interventions. Just as a house needs good and secure foundations to stay standing, CB interventions delivered without a good basis of case formulations which are constructed on a person-by-person basis are likely to crumble and be ineffective.

Subsequent chapters of the text then addressed the practice context, or CBT in action – first looking at interventions for the variety of anxious clients, then for people who are low in mood, who hear voices and have false beliefs, and finally with CBT for people with a diagnosis of Borderline Personality Disorder.

However, the text would not be complete without some consideration of the culture of CBT practice. Happily, it seems impressionistically that practice cultures are becoming increasingly welcoming of, and friendly towards, the uptake of CBT. This being the case, the next section will describe some of the key characteristics of CBT-friendly cultures. Following this, and bringing the book to a close, some pointers will be given for preparing work-cultures and interested individuals within those for the uptake of CBT.

CBT-friendly cultures

It may be useful to begin this section with a little CBT exercise. Continua are often used in the approach to help people shift from a dichotomous thinking style of 'either–or' to consider how they can move along a continuum in a positive direction, or where they are in relation to particular issues. In this context, the continuum can be a useful reference point to locate oneself or to measure progress. Look at the continuum below and mark a cross (X) on the line at the point you think best corresponds to your work setting right now.

100_____0_____100

Absolutely antagonistic　　　　　　　　　　　　　　　　　**Absolutely supportive of**

to the uptake of CBT　　　　　　　　　　　　　　　　　　　**the uptake of CBT**

ACTIVITY *8.1*

If you have put your X to the left of the middle 0, do not despair! The next section will focus on the cultural preparation of workplaces. If your X fell to the right of the 0 above, make a list of the features of your work setting that you think contribute to its CBT-friendliness.

You might have written the following in your CBT-friendly workplace list:

- open to new ideas;
- curious;
- willing to develop;
- supportive of junior staff;
- good, supportive management who deliver what they promise;
- time set aside for study;
- time to spend with clients;
- no obvious possibilities of sabotage, such as individuals who are passive-aggressively negatively disposed towards CBT.

The above points are arguably necessary for the uptake of CBT approaches in mental health. In development of these ideas, Wright and his colleagues (1993) provided well-thought-out and clear accounts of how to create a cognitive milieu in in-patient mental health settings using the model of having a 'primary therapist' in each ward. As the research summary box below will show, this model is not foolproof, but at least allows for increased professionalism in using the approach, service development, and problem solving in relation to associated disadvantages.

RESEARCH SUMMARY

CBT with in-patients: the primary therapist model (Wright, et al., 1993, p62)

Advantages

- *Ward leaders endorse and utilise cognitive therapy.*
- *Rapid introduction of cognitive therapy approaches.*
- *Conducive to outcome research.*
- *Training and supervision encourage high level of competency.*
- *Fits with traditional expectation of patient for treatment from doctor or other primary therapist.*

Disadvantages

- *Possible conflicts with therapists who hold other treatment philosophies.*
- *Patient may be confused if there are competing treatment philosophies.*
- *Power of all staff not fully directed at delivery of cognitive therapy.*
- *Training and supervision are time-consuming and expensive.*
- *Not well suited to other than closed-staff units.*

Work-culture preparation

A culture of defensiveness is often characteristic of workplaces that are not ready to explore the uptake of CBT approaches. Statements such as 'We've tried it before and it doesn't work', 'It's just another fad' or 'It's not our job. We're not therapists' are symptomatic of such cultures. It is also the case that barriers to uptake sometimes follow from false beliefs such as that the approach is easy to learn, and it need not involve the CB practitioner in extended self-reflection, self-development or clinical supervision. I have often come across staff who claim to be 'doing' CBT on the basis of little or no training in the approach, with no clinical supervision and, on further questioning, without having a clear grasp of what CBT is about. Equally, there are individuals who believe that the approach is far too difficult for them to learn or that it belongs solely and exclusively to individuals having advanced psychological education. Clearly, neither of those polarised positions is helpful in the urgent need to disseminate knowledge to underpin the safe and supervised practice of CB knowledge and skills.

Further organisational obstacles include an aversion to risk-taking and a related conformity to traditional structures of rank informing clinical practice. Rank ordering in many mental health settings results in a culture within which practitioners at or near the bottom of the hierarchy are encouraged to 'know their place'. Unless they are personally and collectively tenacious and resourceful, this may inhibit practitioners potentially interested in learning the approach from taking the necessary first steps.

Developing a 'possibility of change' focus

Despite the above, our position is that practitioners can achieve the necessary levels of confidence to create a sympathetic work climate by observing a set of straightforward key cultural change principles (Grant, et al., 2004). Perhaps the first principle that should be emphasised is *don't go it alone*! In a classic organisational change text, Georgiades and Phillimore (1975) argued against the idea of individuals single-handedly attempting to alter work cultures. In the words of these authors, in response to such attempts 'Organisations will, like dragons, eat hero-innovators for breakfast' (p315). Following the advice of these authors, instead of individualistic, misdirected enthusiasm, it would be better to do the following (Grant, et al., 2004):

- *Follow the path of least organisational resistance*   Begin to think about introducing changes in ways that are most likely to mobilise support from organisational members, rather than alienate them from your ideas.

- *Don't focus on lost causes*   Avoid trying to introduce change with people who are extremely antagonistic to the approach or to the notion of changes in work practice. Instead, do the following:

- *Identify allies*   Begin to meet and talk with individuals in your organisation whom you perceive to be the most welcoming on your ideas for change. Then begin to do the following:

- *Work in teams and small groups*   A team approach to CB change initiatives confers many advantages, including solidarity, moral support, problem solving at difficult moments and the development of a good practice culture. Then, collectively, do the following:

- *Check out authority*   On the basis that some individuals will be most influential – either because of their position in the organisation or their interpersonal style – try to indentify and recruit people with clout to your change initiative. Having done this, do the following:

- *Proceed on a realistic timescale*   Change in organisations is a lengthy business and results cannot be achieved hastily. Think in terms of two to three years rather than two to three months.

Good luck!

FURTHER READING

Grant, A, Mills, J, Mulhem, R and Short, N (2004) *Cognitive behavioural therapy in mental health care.* London: Sage Publications Ltd.

Chapter 5 of this text is devoted to establishing CB work cultures, while Chapter 16 addresses organisational factures which impact on, and impede, CBT practice.

USEFUL WEBSITES

www.babcp.com

This is the website of the British Association for Behavioural and Cognitive Psychotherapies. Membership of this association is open to individuals, whether trained or not in the approach. Membership allows people to join the jiscmail discussion list, an excellent resource for those attempting cultural or organisational change in the direction of the uptake of the CBT approach.

Glossary

Behavioural experiments These are central to the practice of contemporary CBT. They refer to helping the client develop and test out specific behavioural strategies in real life. These are designed to help the client *find out* what happens and compare this with their original fears about what might happen. For example, clients with agoraphobic problems who believe they will probably faint if they enter a supermarket would be invited to test this out. Behavioural experiments are carefully constructed to be 'win–win' rather than 'win–lose'. Clients are thus encouraged to learn from each experiment, even when things go wrong in them.

Case formulations Sometimes referred to as 'case conceptualisations', they are a 'map of how someone's problems hang together'. They should be able to explain the relationships between the different elements of a client's difficulties, and enable the individual to see how all elements are linked.

Cognitions This word refers to thoughts and the activity of thinking.

Cognitive distortions These are sometimes called 'cognitive mis-appraisals' or, in extreme cases, 'catastrophic misinterpretations'. Distorted thoughts are inaccurate to the extent to which they do not correspond to what is actually happening in the client's life. 'Catastrophic misinterpretations' refer to worst case thoughts clients may have, such as if my heart beats fast it means that 'I'm about to have a heart attack and die'.

Collaborative empiricism This phrase refers to the client and therapist working closely (collaboratively) together to test out issues in a quasi-scientific manner (empiricism).

Conditioning This word developed from early psychological experiments, either classical or operant, in behavioural psychology. It refers to the process whereby a person or animal learns to respond behaviourally in relation to stimuli presented to them. For example, in early classical conditional studies, dogs learned to salivate to the sound of a bell. In operant conditioning, humans can learn to repeatedly use pub gaming machines in response to intermittent pay-outs from these machines.

Deconstructive and reconstructive questioning Deconstructive questioning refers to questions that are aimed to encourage clients to talk about the past, whereas reconstructive questions are geared to help the client explore possible futures.

Evidence-based healthcare, evidence-based practice Evidence-based healthcare and practice refer to health interventions that are based on robust scientific evidence for their worth. In contrast, non-evidence-based healthcare and practice is based on folklore or custom and practice passed down through generations of healthcare providers.

Intrusions Refer to unwanted thoughts that appear in an individual's consciousness and are resistant to attempts to make them go away. They can be of a sexual, aggressive as well as a nonsense nature. Most of the human adult population experiences intrusive thoughts and consider them meaningless. However, people suffering from obsessional compulsive disorder are likely to view these thoughts in negative terms – as indicating that they are bad people or likely to act on their thoughts (see discussion on thought-action fusion in the text).

Meta-cognition This word simply refers to thinking about thinking.

Methodological This is a term used in the context of conducting or having conducted research. It refers to the general approach taken – for example, 'grounded theory' in qualitative research and 'randomised control trial' in quantitative-experimental research.

Paradigm, paradigmatic The term 'paradigm' or 'paradigmatic' refers to scientific world views. For example, people who conduct quantitative-experimental research would probably subscribe to a *positivist* view of the world, within which the aim of the scientist is to study an external social reality while trying as hard as possible to avoid influencing that which is observed by controlling it. In contrast, qualitative researchers aim to interpret social reality rather than control it. This positions them, therefore, in the interpretive paradigm.

Philosophy of science Closely aligned with paradigms or paradigmatic world views, debates in the philosophy of science refer to assumptions about the nature of reality and what counts as knowledge.

Reattributions Can occur at a verbal, cognitive or behavioural level. The term refers to clients thinking, behaving and talking differently about events as a result of successful CBT or CBT interventions.

Schemas Schemas are the templates for interpreting ourselves, others and the world that all of us have, but take for granted. They are sometimes referred to as 'maladaptive schemas' and 'inner working models' in the context of the internal template or map that Borderline Personality Disorder clients have of themselves and others. Schemas are considered to relate early childhood experiences with significant others. In the case of individuals with personality disorder problems, such experiences are likely to have been toxic.

References

Abramson, LY, Seligman, MEP and Teasdale, J (1978) Learned helplessness in humans: Critique and reformulation. *Journal of Abnormal Psychology*, 87: 49–94.

Andrews, G and Henderson, S (eds) (2000) *Unmet need in psychiatry: Problems, resources, responses.* Cambridge: Cambridge University Press.

Antony, MM, Orsillo, SM and Roemer, L (eds) (2001) *Practitioner's guide to empirically based measures of anxiety.* New York: Kluwer Academic/Plenum Publishers.

(APA) American Psychiatric Association (1994) *Diagnostic and statistical manual of mental disorders (DSM IV).* 4th edition. Washington DC: APA.

(APA) American Psychiatric Association (2000) *Diagnostic and statistical manual of mental disorders (DSM IV).* 4th edition, text revision. Washington DC: APA.

Atha, C (1992) The role of the CPN with clients who deliberately harm themselves. In Brooker, C (ed) *Community psychiatric nursing: A research perspective.* London: Chapman and Hall.

Bandura, A (1977) *Social learning theory.* Englewood Cliffs, NJ: Prentice-Hall.

Barker, P (1992) *Severe depression: The practitioner's guide.* London: Chapman and Hall.

Barlow, DG, Levitt, JT and Bufka, LF (1999) The dissemination of empirically supported treatments: A view to the future. *Behaviour Research and Therapy,* 37: 147–62.

Beck, AT (1976) *Cognitive therapy and the emotional disorders.* London: Penguin Books.

Beck, AT (1996) *Beck depression inventory.* San Antonio: The Psychological Corporation.

Beck, AT and Emery, G (1985) *Anxiety disorders and phobias: A cognitive perspective.* New York: Basic Books.

Beck, AT, Freeman, A and Davis, D (eds) (2003) *Cognitive therapy of personality disorders.* Revised edition. New York: The Guilford Press.

Beck, AT, Epstein, N, Brown, G and Steer, RA (1988) An inventory for measuring clinical anxiety: Psychometric properties. *Journal of Consulting and Clinical Psychology,* 56: 893–97.

Beck, AT, Rush, AJ, Shaw, BF and Emery, G (1979) *Cognitive therapy of depression.* New York: The Guilford Press.

Beck, AT, Freeman, A, Pretzer, J, Davis, DD, Fleming, B, Ottaviani, R, Beck, J, Simon, JM, Padesky, C, Meyer, J and Trexler, L (1990) *Cognitive therapy of personality disorders.* New York: The Guilford Press.

Beck, J S (1995) *Cognitive therapy: Basics and beyond.* New York: Guilford Press.

Beech, I (2003) The person who experiences depression. In Barker, P (ed) *Psychiatric and mental health nursing, the craft of caring.* London: Arnold.

Bendall, E (1976) Learning for reality. *Journal of Advanced Nursing,* 1: 3–9.

Bennett-Levy, J, Butler, G, Fennell, M, Hackman, A, Mueller, M and Westbrook, D (2004) *Oxford guide to behavioural experiments in cognitive therapy.* Oxford and New York: Oxford University Press.

Bentall, R (1990) *Reconstructing schizophrenia*. London: Routledge.

Birchwood, M, Fowler, D and Jackson, C (2000) *Early intervention in psychosis*. Chichester: Wiley.

Bolsover, N (2002) Commentary: The 'evidence' is weaker than claimed. *British Medical Journal*, 324: 288–94.

Boyle, M (1990) *Schizophrenia – A scientific delusion?* London: Routledge.

British Association for Behavioural and Cognitive Psychotherapies (BABCP) (2007) *Guidelines for good practice*.

British Association for Behavioural and Cognitive Psychotherapies (2009) *Standards of conduct, performance and ethics in the practice of behavioural and cognitive psychotherapies*. Available at: **www.babcp.com**

Brooker, C, Gournay, K, O'Halloran, P, Bailey, D and Saul C (2002) Mapping training to support the implementation of the National Service Framework for mental health. *Journal of Mental Health*, 11(1): 103–16.

Brown, G and Harris, T (1978) *The social origins of depression: A study of psychiatric disorder in women*. London: Tavistock.

Bruce, M (2002) Psychosocial risk factors for depressive disorders in late life. *Biological Psychiatry*, 52: 175–84.

Burns, D (1990) *The feeling good handbook*. New York and London: Plume.

Casey, LM, Oei, TPS and Newcombe, PA (2004) An integrated model of panic disorder: The role of positive and negative cognitions. *Clinical Psychology Review*, 24(5): 529–55.

Castillo, H, Allen, L and Coxhead, N (2001) The hurtfulness of a diagnosis: User research about personality disorder. *Mental Health Practice*, 4(9): 16–19.

Cautela, LR (1973) Covert processes and behaviour modification. *Journal of Mental and Nervous Diseases*, 157: 27–36.

Centre for Economic Performance (2006) *The Depression Report. A new deal for depression and anxiety disorders*. London: The London School of Economics and Political Science. Website: **http://cep.lse.ac.uk/research/mentalhealth**

Chadwick, P, Birchwood, M and Trower, P (1996) *Cognitive therapy for delusions, voices and paranoia*. Chichester: Wiley.

Chambless, DL, Beck, AT, Gracely, EJ and Grisham, JR (2000) Relationship of cognitions to fear of somatic symptoms: A test of the cognitive theory of panic. *Depression and Anxiety*, 11: 1–9.

Clark, DM (1986) A cognitive model of panic. *Behaviour Research and Therapy*, 24: 461–70.

Clark, DM and Beck, AT (2009) *Cognitive therapy for anxiety disorders: Science and practice*. New York: Guilford.

Clarke, L (1999) Nursing in search of a science: The rise and rise of the new nurse brutalism. *Mental Health Care*, 21(8): 270–72.

Clarke, L and Flanagan, T (2003) *Institutional breakdown. Exploring mental health nursing practice in acute inpatient settings*. Salisbury: APS Publishing.

CSIP (2009) Website: **www.csip.org.uk**

Davidson, K (2007) *Cognitive therapy for personality disorders: A guide for clinicians*. 2nd edition. Hove: Routledge.

Davidson, K, Sharp, M and Halford, J (2010) CBT for antisocial and borderline personality disorder. In Grant, A, Townend, M, Mulhern, R and Short, N (2010) *Cognitive behavioural therapy in mental health care.* 2nd edition. London: Sage Publications Ltd.

Davidson, K, Norrie, J, Tyrer, P, Gumley, A, Tata, P, Murray, H and Palmer, S (2006) The effectiveness of cognitive behaviour therapy for borderline personality disorder: Results from the BOSCOT trial. *Journal of Personality Disorders,* 20(5): 450–65.

Deale, A (1997) Cognitive behaviour therapy for chronic fatigue syndrome: A randomised controlled trial. *American Journal of Psychiatry,* 154(3): 404–14.

Department of Health (DoH) (1994) *Working in partnership: A collaborative approach to care. Report of the mental health nursing review team.* London: HMSO.

Department of Health (DoH) (1996) *NHS psychotherapy services in England: Review of strategic policy.* London: Department of Health.

Department of Health (DoH) (1998) *Modernising mental health services: Safe, sound and supportive.* London: The Stationery Office.

Department of Health (DoH) (1999) *National Service framework for mental health.* London: Department of Health.

Department of Health (DoH) (2001) *Mental health policy implementation guide.* London: Department of Health.

Department of Health (DoH) (2004) *The NHS knowledge and skills framework (KSF) and the development review process.* **www.dh.gov.uk**

Department of Health (DoH) (2006) *Recruitment and retention of mental health nurses: Good practice guide. The chief nursing officer's review of mental health nursing.* London: Department of Health.

Department of Health (DoH) (2007a) *The competences required to deliver effective cognitive and behavioural therapy for people with depression and with anxiety disorders.* London: Department of Health.

Department of Health (DoH) (2007b) *Improving access to psychological therapies: Specification for the commissioner-led Pathfinder programme.* **www.dh.gov.uk**

Department of Health (DoH) (2007c) *Improving access to psychological therapies (IAPT) programme. Computerised cognitive behavioural therapy (cCBT) implementation guidance.* **www.dh.gov.uk**

Dimidjian, S, Hollan, SD and Dobson, KS (2006) Randomised trial of behavioural activation, cognitive therapy, and antidepressant medication in the acute treatment of adults with major depression. *Journal of Consulting and Clinical Psychology,* 74(4): 658–70.

Dobson, KS and Dozois DJA (2001) Historical and philosophical bases of the cognitive-behavioural therapies. In Dobson, KS (ed) *Handbook of cognitive behavioural therapies.* 2nd edition. New York and London: The Guilford Press.

Dryden, W (ed) (2007) *Dryden's handbook of individual therapy.* 5th edition. London: Sage Publications Ltd.

Du, L, Faludi, G, Palkovits, M, Bakish, D and Hrdina, P (2001) Serotonergic genes and suicidality. *Crisis,* 22: 54–60.

Duggan, C, Huband, N, Smailagic, N, Ferriter, M and Adams, C (2007) The use of psychological treatments for people with personality disorder: A systematic review of randomised controlled trials. *Personality and Mental Health,* 1: 95–125.

Duncan-Grant, A (1999a) CBT training for mental health nurses: ENB650. Part one. *Mental Health Practice,* 2(7): 10–12.

Duncan-Grant, A (1999b) Misrepresentation, stereotyping, and acknowledging bias in science: Responses to Liam Clarke. *Mental Health Care,* 21(10): 336–7.

Eastwick, Z and Grant, A (2005) The treatment of people with 'borderline personality disorder': A cause for concern? *Mental Health Practice*, 8(7): 38–40.

Eaton, WW, Thara, R, Federman, E and Tien, A (1998) Remission and relapse in schizophrenia: The Madras Longitudinal Study. *The Journal of Nervous & Mental Disease*, 186(6): 357–63.

Edwards, S and Salkovskis, PM (2006) An experimental demonstration that fear, but not disgust, is associated with return of fear in phobias. *Journal of Anxiety Disorders*, 20: 58–71.

Egan, G (1986) *The skilled helper. A systematic approach to effective helping.* 3rd edition. Pacific Grove, CA: Brooks/Cole.

Ehlers, A and Clark, DM (2000) A cognitive model of post-traumatic stress disorder. *Behaviour Research and Therapy*, 38: 319–45.

Ellis, A (1962) *Reason and Emotion in Psychotherapy.* Secaucus, NJ: Lyle Stuart.

Ellis, A, Gordon, J, Neenan, M and Palmer, S (2001) *Stress counselling: A rational emotive behaviour approach.* London: Sage Publications Ltd.

Fennell, MJV (1999) *Overcoming low self-esteem: A self-help guide using cognitive behavioural techniques*. London: Robinson.

Fennell, M (2006) *Overcoming low self-esteem self help course, a 3 part programme based on cognitive behavioural techniques.* London: Constable & Robinson.

Fineman, S (ed) (1996) *Emotion in organisations.* London: Sage Publications Ltd.

Foa, EB and Kozak, MJ (1986) Emotional processing of fear: Exposure to corrective information. *Psychological Bulletin*, 99(1): 20–35.

Foa, EB and Rothbaum, BO (1998) *Treating the trauma of rape: Cognitive behavioural therapy for PTSD.* New York and London: The Guilford Press.

Foa, EB and Steketee, G (1989) Behavioural/cognitive conceptualizations in post-traumatic stress disorder. *Behavior Therapy*, 20: 155–76.

Gamble, C and Brennan, G (eds) (2000) *Working with serious mental illness: A manual for clinical practice.* London: Balliere Tindall in association with the Royal College of Nursing, Harcourt.

Garety, PA, Kuipers, E, Fowler, D, Freeman, D and Bebbington, PE (2001) A cognitive model of the positive symptoms of psychosis. *Psychological Medicine*, 31: 189–95.

Garland, A (1996) Cognitive therapy for depression. *Mental Health Nursing,* 16(3): 28–31.

Garlow, SJ, Musselman, DL and Nemeroff, CB (1999) The neurochemistry of mood disorders: Clinical studies. In Charney, DS, Nestler, EJ and Bunney, BS (eds) *Neurobiology of mental illness.* New York and Oxford: Oxford University Press.

Georgiades, NJ and Phillimore, L (1975) The myth of the hero-innovator and alternative strategies for organizational change. In Kiernan, CC and Woodward, FP (eds) *Behavioural modification with the severely retarded.* London: Associated Scientific Publishers.

Giesen-Bloo, J, van Dyck, R, Spinhoven, P, van Tilburg, W, Dirksen, C, van Asselt, T, Kremers, I, Nadort, M and Arntz, A (2006) Outpatient psychotherapy for borderline personality disorder: Randomized trial of schema-focused therapy vs transference-focused psychotherapy. *Archives of General Psychiatry*, 63: 649–58.

Goffman, E (1969) *The presentation of self in everyday life.* Reading: Pelican.

Goldberg, D and Hillier, V (1978) A scaled version of the General Health Questionnaire. *Psychological Medicine*, 9: 139–46.

Goldstein, AJ and Chambless, DL (1978) A re-analysis of agoraphobia. *Behavior Therapy*, 9: 47–59.

Gournay, K (1997) Body dysmorphic disorder: Pilot randomised controlled trial of treatment; implications for nurse therapy research and practice. *Clinical Effectiveness Nursing*, 1(46): 38–43.

Grant, A and Mills, J (2000) The great going nowhere show: Structural power and mental health nurses. *Mental Health Practice*, 4(3): 14–16.

Grant, A, Mills, J, Mulhern, R and Short, N (2004) *Cognitive behavioural therapy in mental health care.* London: Sage Publications Ltd.

Grant, A, Townend, M, Mills, J and Cockx, A (2008) *Assessment and case formulation in cognitive behavioural therapy.* London: Sage Publications Ltd.

Grant, A, Townend, M, Mulhern, R and Short N (2010) *Cognitive behavioural therapy in mental health care.* 2nd edition. London: Sage Publications Ltd.

Greenberger, D and Padesky, CA (1995) *Mind over mood: Change how you feel by changing the way you think.* New York: Guilford Press.

Grippo, A and Johnson, A (2002) Biological mechanisms in the relationship between depression and heart disease. *Neuroscience Biobehavioural Review*, 26: 941–62.

Gumley, A, O'Grady, M, McNay, L, Reilly, K, Power, K and Norrie, J (2003) Early intervention for relapse in schizophrenia: Results of a 12 month randomised controlled trial of cognitive behavioural therapy. *Psychological Medicine*, 33: 419–31.

Hackmann, A (2004) Panic disorder and agoraphobia. In Bennett-Levy, J, Butler, G, Fennell, M, Hackman, A, Mueller, M and Westbrook, D (eds) *Oxford guide to behavioural experiments in cognitive therapy*. Oxford and New York: Oxford University Press.

Haddock, G, Bentall, RP and Slade, PD (1996) Psychological treatment of auditory hallucinations: Focusing or distraction? In Haddock, G and Slade, PD (eds) *Cognitive–behavioural interventions with psychotic disorders.* London: Routledge.

Hall, PL and Tarrier, N (2003) The cognitive-behavioural treatment of low self-esteem in psychotic patients: A pilot study. *Behaviour Research and Therapy*, 41: 317–32.

Haque, MS, Nolan, P, Dyke, R and Khan, I (2002) The work and values of mental health nurses observed. *Journal of Psychiatric and Mental Health Nursing*, 9(6): 673–80.

Hawton, K, Salkovskis, PM, Kirk, J and Clark, DM (eds) (1989) *Cognitive behaviour therapy for psychiatric problems: A practical guide.* New York: Oxford University Press.

Heron, J (2000) *Helping the client. A creative practical guide.* London: Sage Publications Ltd.

Holmes, J (2002) All you need is cognitive behaviour therapy? *British Medical Journal*, 324: 288–94.

Jackson, H, McGorry, P, Edwards, J, Hulbert, C, Henry, L, Harrigan, S, Dudgeon, P, Francey, S, Maude, D, Cocks, J, Killacky, E and Power, P (2005) A controlled trial of cognitively oriented psychotherapy for early psychosis (COPE) with four-year follow-up readmission data. *Psychological Medicine*, 35(9): 1295–306.

Jacobson, NS, Martell, CR and Truax, PA (1996) A component analysis of cognitive behavioural treatment for depression. *Journal of Consulting and Clinical Psychology*, 64(2): 295–304.

Keller, MC and Ness, RM (2005) Is low mood an adaptation? Evidence for subtypes with symptoms that match precipitants. *Journal of Affective Disorders*, 86: 27–35.

Kelly, G (1955) *The psychology of personal constructs, Vols I and II.* New York: Norton.

Kendrick, T, Burns, T, Garland, C, Greenwood, N and Smith, P (2000) Are specialist mental health services being targeted on the most needy patients? The effects of setting up special services in general practices. *British Journal of General Practice*, 50: 121–6.

Kingdon, D, Vincent, S, Kinoshita, Y and Turkington, (D) (2008) Destigmatising schizophrenia: Does changing terminology reduce negative attitudes? *Psychiatric Bulletin*, 32(11): 419–23.

Kirk, J and Rouf, K (2004) Specific phobias. In Bennett-Levy, J, Butler, G, Fennell, M, Hackman, A, Mueller, M and Westbrook, D (eds) *Oxford guide to behavioural experiments in cognitive therapy.* Oxford and New York: Oxford University Press.

Kuipers, E, Garety, P, Fowler, D, Dunn, G, Bebbington, P, Freeman, D and Hadley, C (1997) London–East Anglia randomised controlled trial of cognitive-behavioural therapy for psychosis. I: effects of the treatment phase. *The British Journal of Psychiatry*, 171: 319–27.

Kuyken, W, Dalgleish, T and Holden, ER (2007) Advances in cognitive-behavioural therapy for unipolar depression. *The Canadian Journal of Psychiatry*, 52(1): 5–12.

Larkin, J and Simon, H (1987) Why a diagram is (sometimes) worth ten thousand words. *Cognitive Science*, 11: 65–99.

Lazarus, RS and Folkman, S (1984) *Stress, appraisal, and coping.* New York: Springer.

Leahy, RL (2003) *Cognitive therapy techniques: A practitioner's guide.* New York: Guilford Press.

Leahy, RL and Holland SJ (2000) *Treatment plans and interventions for depression and anxiety disorders.* New York: Guilford Press.

Lecomte, T, Cyr, M, Lesage, AD, Wilde, J, Leclerc, C and Richard, N (1999) Efficacy of a self esteem module in the empowerment of individuals with schizophrenia. *The Journal of Nervous and Mental Disease*, 187: 406–13.

Lewinsohn, PM, Weinstein, M and Shaw, D (1969) Depression: A clinical research approach, in Rubin, RD and Frank, CM (eds) *Advances in behavior therapy.* New York: Academic Press.

Linehan, MM (1987) Dialectical behaviour therapy for borderline personality disorder: Theory and method. *Bulletin of the Menninger Clinic*, 51: 261–76.

Lovell, K and Richards, D (1995) Behavioural treatment of PTSD. *British Journal of Nursing,* 4(16): 934–6.

Lovibond, SH and Lovibond, PF (1995) *Manual for the depression anxiety stress scales.* 2nd edition. Sydney: Psychology Foundation.

Maben, J, Latter, S and Macleod Clark, J (2006) The theory-practice gap: Impact of professional-bureaucratic work conflict on newly-qualified nurses. *Journal of Advanced Nursing,* 55(4): 465–77.

Mahoney, MJ and Arnkoff, DB (1978) Cognitive and self-control therapies. In Garfield, SL and Bergin, AE (eds) *Handbook of psychotherapy and behavior change.* 2nd edition. New York: Wiley.

Marano, HE (2002) The different faces of depression. *Psychology Today Magazine.* Sussex Publishers, LLC, New York, July/August.

Marien, B (2005) How to explain the causes and treatment of depression. Talking to patients. *Prescriber,* 5 September.

Marks, IM (1980) *Living with fear, understanding and coping with anxiety.* Maidenhead: McGraw-Hill.

Marks, M (2003) Cognitive therapy for obsessive-compulsive disorder. In Menzies, RG and de Silva, P (eds) *Obsessive-compulsive disorder: Theory, research and treatment.* Chichester: Wiley.

Meichenbaum, D (1997) *Treating posttraumatic stress disorder: A handbook and practice manual.* Chichester: Wiley.

Mills, J, Mulhern, R, Short, N and Grant, A (2004a) Working with people who hear voices and have strange beliefs. In Grant, A, Mills, J, Mulhern, R and Short, N (eds) *Cognitive behavioural therapy in mental health care.* London: Sage Publications Ltd.

Mills, J, Mulhern, R, Short, N and Grant, A (2004b) Working with people who have complex emotional and relationship difficulties (borderlines or people?). In Grant, A, Mills, J, Mulhern, R and Short, N (eds) *Cognitive behavioural therapy in mental health care.* London: Sage Publications Ltd.

Mineka, S and Zinbarg, R (2006) A contemporary learning theory perspective on the etiology of anxiety disorders. *American Psychologist,* 61(1): 10–26.

Moorey, S (2007) Cognitive therapy. In Dryden, W (ed) *Dryden's handbook of individual therapy.* 5th edition. London: Sage Publications Ltd.

Morgan G (1997) *Images of organisation.* 2nd edition. Thousand Oaks, CA: Sage Publications Inc.

Morrison, AP, French, P, Walford, L, Lewis, SW, Kilcommons, A, Green, J, Parker, S and Bentall, RP (2004) Cognitive therapy for the prevention of psychosis in people at ultra-high risk. Randomised controlled trial. *British Journal of Psychiatry,* 185: 291–97.

Mowrer, OH (1960) *Learning theory and behaviour.* New York: Wiley.

Nathan, PE, Gorman, JM and Salkind, NJ (1999) *Treating mental disorders: A guide to what works.* New York: Oxford University Press.

National Institute for Health and Clinical Excellence (NICE). Website: **www.nice.org.uk**

Nemeroff, CB (1998) The neurobiology of depression. *Scientific American,* 278: 42–9.

Nemeroff, C (2004) Neurobiological consequences of childhood trauma. *Journal of Clinical Psychiatry,* 65: 18–28.

Newell, R and Gournay, K (1994) British nurses in behavioural psychotherapy: A 20-year follow-up. *Journal of Advanced Nursing,* 20: 53–60.

Newell, R and Gournay, K (eds) (2000) *Mental health nursing: An evidence-based approach.* London: Churchill Livingstone.

Nuechterlein, KH, Dawson, ME, Ventura, J, Gitlin, M, Subotnik, KL, Snyder, KS, Mintz, J and Bartzokis, G (2007) The vulnerability/stress model of schizophrenic relapse: A longitudinal study. *Acta Psychiatrica Scandinavica,* 89: 58–64.

Obsessive Compulsive Cognitions Working Group (1997) Cognitive assessment of obsessive-compulsive disorder. *Behaviour Research and Therapy,* 35(7): 667–81.

O'Carroll, M and Park, A (2007) *Essential mental health nursing skills.* London: Mosby Elsevier.

Padesky, CA (1993) *Socratic questioning: Changing minds or guiding discovery.* A keynote address delivered at the European Congress of Behavioural and Cognitive Therapies. 24 September, London.

Padesky, C (2–3 October 1998) When there's not enough time: Cognitive therapy innovations. Workshop handout. Imperial College, London.

Padesky, CA and Mooney, KA (1990) Clinical tip: Presenting the cognitive model to clients. *International Cognitive Therapy Newsletter.* 6: 13–14. Available from **www.padesky.com/clinicalcorner/pubs.htm**

Paris, J and Zweig-Frank, H (2001) A 27-year follow-up of patients with borderline personality disorder. *Comprehensive Psychiatry,* 42: 482–87.

Pfeffer, J (1981) *Power in organisations.* Marshfield, MA: Pitman.

Pretzer, J (1990) Borderline personality disorder. In Beck, AT, Freeman, A, Pretzer, J, Davis, DD, Fleming, B, Ottaviani, R, Beck, J, Simon, JM, Padesky, C, Meyer, J and Trexler, L (eds) *Cognitive therapy of personality disorders.* New York: The Guilford Press.

Prien, R and Kupfer, D (1986) Continuation drug therapy for major depressive episodes: How long should it be maintained? *American Journal of Psychiatry*, 143: 18–23 (B11).

Purdon, C and Clark, DA (1993) Obsessive intrusive thoughts in nonclinical subjects. Part I. Content and relation with depressive, anxious and obsessional symptoms. *Behaviour Research and Therapy*, 31(8): 713–20.

Purser, RE and Cabana, S (1998) *The self-managing organisation: How leading companies are transforming the work of teams for real impact.* New York: Free Press, Simon & Shuster Inc.

Rachman, SJ (1996) Trends in cognitive and behavioural therapies. In Salkovskis, PM (ed) *Trends in cognitive and behavioural therapies.* Chichester: John Wiley.

Rachman, S and de Silva, P (1978) Abnormal and normal obsessions. *Behaviour Research and Therapy*, 16: 233–48.

Raphael, B (1996) *The anatomy of bereavement.* London: Routledge.

Richards, D (2007) High-volume psychological therapies: Data from the first year of the Doncaster increasing access to psychological therapies demonstration site. Paper given at the BABCP Annual Conference and Workshops. University of Sussex, 12–14 September.

Rutter, M (1993) *Developing minds: Challenge and continuity across the life span.* New York: Basic Books.

Salkovskis, PM (1985) Obsessional-compulsive problems: A cognitive-behavioural analysis. *Behaviour Research and Therapy*, 23(5): 571–83.

Salkovskis, PM (1989) Cognitive-behavioural actors and the persistence of intrusive thoughts in obsessional problems. *Behaviour Research and Therapy*, 27: 677–82.

Salkovskis, PM (1991) The importance of behaviour in the maintenance of anxiety and panic: A cognitive account. *Behavioural Psychotherapy*, 19: 6–19.

Salkovskis, PM (1996) The cognitive approach to anxiety: Threat beliefs, safety-seeking behaviour, and the special case of health anxiety and obsessions. In Salkovskis, PM (ed) *Frontiers of cognitive therapy.* New York and London: The Guilford Press.

Salkovskis, PM (2004) Psychological treatment of obsessive-compulsive disorder: *Psychiatry*, 3(6): 68–72.

Salkovskis, PM (2007) Cognitive behavioural treatment for panic. *Psychiatry*, 6(5): 193–7.

Salkovskis, PM and McGuire, J (2003) Cognitive-behavioural theory of obsessive-compulsive disorder. In Menzies, RG and de Silva, P (eds) *Obsessive compulsive disorder: Theory, research and treatment.* Chichester: Wiley.

Salkovskis, PM and Warwick, H (1986) Morbid preoccupations, health anxiety and reassurance: A cognitive-behavioural approach to hypochondriasis. *Behaviour Research and Therapy*, 24: 597–602.

Salkovskis, PMA, Hackman, A, Wells, A, Gelder, MG and Clark, DM (2007) Belief disconfirmation versus habituation approaches to situational exposure in panic disorder and agoraphobia: A pilot study. *Behaviour Research and Therapy*, 45 (5): 877–85.

Sanders, D and Wills, F (2005) *Cognitive therapy, an introduction.* 2nd edition. London: Sage Publications Ltd.

Schneider, K (1959) *Clinical psychopathology.* New York: Grune and Stratton.

SCMH (Sainsbury Centre for Mental Health) (2000) *The capable practitioner. A framework and list of the practitioner capabilities required to implement the National Service Framework for Mental Health.* London: SCMH.

Shafran, R, Thordarson, DS and Rachman, S (1996) Thought-action fusion in obsessive compulsive disorder. *Journal of Anxiety Disorders*, 10(5): 379–91.

Short, N, Kitchiner, NJ and Curran, J (2004) Unreliable evidence. *Journal of Psychiatric and Mental Health Nursing*, 11(1): 106–11.

Silk, KR (2008) Augmenting psychotherapy for borderline personality disorder: The STEPPS program. Editorial. *American Journal of Psychiatry*, 165: 413–15.

Silver, AD, Sanders, D, Morrison, N and Cowey, C (2004) Health anxiety. In Bennett-Levy, J, Butler, G, Fennell, M, Hackman, A, Mueller, M and Westbrook, D (2004) *Oxford guide to behavioural experiments in cognitive therapy*. Oxford and New York: Oxford University Press.

Skodol, AE, Gunderson, JG, Shea, MT, McGlashan, TH, Morey, LC, Sanislow, CA, Bender, DS, Grilo, CM, Zanarini, MC, Yen, S, Pagano, ME and Stout, RL (2005) The collaborative longitudinal personality disorders study (CLPS): Overview and implications. *Journal of Personality Disorders*, 19(5): 487–504.

Spigset, O and Martensson, B (1999) Fortnightly review: Drug treatment of depression. *British Medical Journal*, 318: 1188–91.

Steel, C (2008) Cognitive behavioural therapy for psychosis: Current evidence and future directions. *Behavioural and Cognitive Psychotherapy*, 36: 705–12.

Strunk, DR and DeRubeis, RJ (2001) Cognitive therapy for depression: A review of its efficacy. *Journal of Cognitive Psychotherapy*, 15(4): 289–97.

Swofford, CD, Kasckow, JW, Scheller-Gilkey, G and Inderbitzen, LB (1996) Substance use: A powerful predictor of relapse in schizophrenia. *Schizophrenia Research*, 20(1): 145–51.

Szasz, TS (1960) The myth of mental illness. *American Psychologist*, 15: 113–18.

Thomas, A, Kalaria, R and O'Brien, J (2004) Depression and vascular disease: What is the relationship? *Journal Affective Disorders*, 79: 81–5.

Thorpe, SJ and Salkovskis, PM (1995) Phobic beliefs: Do cognitive factors play a role in specific phobias? *Behaviour Research and Therapy*, 33(7): 805–16.

Trower, P, Casey, A and Dryden, W (1995) *Cognitive behavioural counselling in action*. 3rd edition. London: Sage Publications Ltd.

Tschudin, V (1987) *Counselling skills for nurses*. 2nd edition. London: Bailliere Tindall.

UKCC (1986) *Project 2000: A new preparation for practice*. London: UKCC.

UKCC (1999) *Fitness for practice. The UKCC commission for nursing and midwifery education*. London: UKCC.

Veale, D and Willson, R (2007) *Manage your mood – How to use behavioural activation techniques to overcome depression*. London: Robinson.

Wakefield, JC, Schmitz, MF, First, MB and Horwitz, AV (2007) Extending the bereavement exclusion for major depression to other losses: Evidence from the National Comorbidity Survey. *Archives of General Psychiatry*, April, 64(4): 433–40.

Warwick, HM and Salkovskis, PM (1990) Hypochondriasis. *Behaviour research and therapy*, 28: 105–17.

Wells, A (1997) *Cognitive therapy of anxiety disorders: A practice manual and conceptual guide*. Chichester: John Wiley.

Wells, A (2002) *Emotional disorders and metacognition: Innovative cognitive therapy*. Chichester: John Wiley & Sons.

Wells, A (2009) *Metacognitive therapy for anxiety and depression.* New York and London: Guilford Press.

Wells, A and Cartwright-Hatton, S (2004) A short form of the metacognitions questionnaire: Properties of the MCQ-30. *Behaviour Research and Therapy*, 42(4): 385–96.

Wells, A and Sembi, S (2004) Metacognitive therapy for PTSD: A preliminary investigation of a new brief treatment. *Journal of Behavior Therapy and Experimental Psychiatry*, 35(4): 307–18.

Whittington, D and McLaughlin, C (2000) Finding time for patients and exploration of nurses' time allocation in an acute psychiatric setting. *Journal of Psychiatric and Mental Health Nursing*, 7: 259–68.

Williams, M, Teasdale, J, Segal, Z and Kabat-Zinn, J (2007) *The mindful way through depression.* New York and London: The Guilford Press.

World Health Organisation (WHO) (1992) *ICD-10: The ICD-10 classification of mental and behavioural disorders: Clinical descriptions and diagnostic guidelines.* World Health Organisation.

World Health Organisation (WHO) (2001) *World Health Report 2001, Mental health; New understanding, new hope.* Geneva: World Health Organisation.

Wright, JH, Thase, ME, Ludgate, JW and Beck, AT (1993) The cognitive milieu: Structure and process. In Wright, JH, Thase, ME, Ludgate, JW and Beck, AT (eds) *Cognitive therapy with inpatients. Developing a cognitive milieu.* New York and London: The Guilford Press.

Young, J (1990) *Cognitive therapy for personality disorders: A schema-focused approach.* 3rd edition. Sarasota, FL: Professional Resource Exchange.

Young, J and Behary, WT (1998) Schema-focused therapy for personality disorders. In Tarrier, N, Wells, A and Haddock, G (eds) *Treating complex cases.* Chichester: Wiley.

Young, J, Klosko, J and Weishaar, ME (2003) *Schema therapy, a practitioners guide.* New York: The Guilford Press.

Zanarini, MC, Frankenburg, FR, Hennen, J and Silk, KR (2003) Longitudinal course of borderline psychopathology: 6-year prospective study. *American Journal of Psychiatry*, 160: 274–2.

Zubin, J and Spring, B (1977) Vulnerability – a new view of schizophrenia. *Journal of Abnormal Psychology*, 86(2): 103–26.

Index